ELEMENTS OF THE **EXTRAORDINARY**

Do-It-Yourself
FENG SHUI

Take Charge of your Destiny !

ELEMENTS OF THE **EXTRAORDINARY**

Do-It-Yourself FENG SHUI

Take Charge of your Destiny !

BY WU YING
Illustrated by Paul Davies

ELEMENT
CHILDREN'S BOOKS

SHAFTESBURY, DORSET · BOSTON, MASSACHUSETTS · MELBOURNE, VICTORIA

Dedicated to three teachers from three Chinas
Li Ruru, Yip Po Ching, and Shu Wen Wu

© Element Children's Books 1998
Text © Wu Ying 1998
Illustrations © Paul Davies 1998

First published in Great Britain in 1998 by Element Children's Books,
Shaftesbury, Dorset SP7 8BP

Published in the USA in 1998 by Element Books Inc.
PO Box 830, Boston MA

Published in Australia in 1998 by Element Books
and distributed by Penguin Books Australia Ltd,
487 Maroondah Highway, Ringwood, Victoria 3134

British Library Cataloguing in Publication data available.
Library of Congress Cataloging in Publication data available.

ISBN 1 901881 35 0

Cover design by Ness Wood
Printed and bound in Great Britain by
Creative Print and Design (Wales), Ebbw Vale

Contents

Chapter 1   Family Fortunes   6

Chapter 2   Welcome to the Real World   13

Chapter 3   The World Beyond   16

Chapter 4   Stuff about Dragons   27

Chapter 5   Qi and the Natural World   33

Chapter 6   Feng Shui at Home   38

Chapter 7   The Magic Octagon   49

Chapter 8   Elements and Colors   60

Chapter 9   Elements and the Chinese Zodiac   69

Chapter 10 Bedroom Feng Shui   79

Chapter 11 Feng Shui at School   91

Chapter 12 Back to the Real World   99

Glossary of Magical Influences   104

Family Fortunes

Feng shui (pronounced to rhyme with "tongue sway") literally means "wind and water." You can be touched by these elements, but you can't hold them in your hands. These are only two of the many forces of Nature that play a part in our lives, and if you understand more about the way they work, you can improve your life for the better. Feng shui is an ancient Chinese art that manages to combine astrology with home decorating, geography with mythology, and history with magic.

I had my first encounter with feng shui several years ago when I had to stay at home to let in the feng shui man. I had no idea what he was supposed to do. All I knew was that no one was ever scared of the gas man or the guy who came to read the electricity meter, but my mother ran around the house frantically tidying up all the mess before the feng shui man arrived. It didn't look messy to the rest of us, but she said that feng shui men were very particular.

I'd seen him from my window. He walked up and down the street a couple of times, obviously looking for someone's address.

I thought he was an insurance salesman or something, so I couldn't believe my ears when I heard him ringing *our* doorbell.

"Is this the Wu household?" he asked politely.

"It might be," I said testily. "Are you the feng shui man?"

"I might be," he smiled.

"You don't look like a sorcerer."

The man kept on smiling. "What were you expecting, kid? Sandals and a pointy hat?"

It was the "kid" bit that really annoyed me, but I guess he was right. When Dad said I'd have to stay inside to let in the feng shui man, I'd been looking out of the window for something spectacular. I don't know, maybe a man on a flying carpet, a squadron of dragons trying to squash into the backyard, a giant god throwing thunderbolts. Something like that, anyway. Whatever I'd been looking for, I'd never have guessed in a  million years he'd turn up wearing a run-of-the-mill suit. He was carrying a briefcase, too.

"All right," I said. "If you're a feng shui man, tell me how I'm going to do in the test tomorrow."

"I don't predict the future," he laughed.

"What do you do, then?"

"I change it."

He strode into the hall and looked around him.

"I had trouble finding your house," he said. Excuses, excuses. It wasn't my fault he was ten minutes late.

"That's because it's set back a little from the street," I explained.

"That's good," he said.

"Because it made you late?"

"No. Because it makes *you* lucky."

"Oh," I said, more or less running out of angry things to say.

"I guess your Dad didn't tell you why I'm here," he said. "It's my job to make sure you and your family get all the good fortune they deserve, and I do that by checking that your house is lucky."

"Yeah, right."

"*Yeah!*" he said. "Right! You'd better believe it, kid." He was busy taking papers out of his briefcase. They looked suspiciously like the blueprints of our house.

"Houses are just there," I scowled. "You can't have a lucky house."

"Really?" said the feng shui man. "You seem to know a lot about it."

I shrugged.

"So perhaps you can tell me," he said, with a smile, "why you aren't doing as well as your brother at school?"

I was flabbergasted. How did he know that?

"*Your* room's at the front of the house, right?" he continued.

"Yeah ..."

"Just a little closer to the noise of a busy street ...?"

"I suppose so."

"Do you have trouble sleeping at night?"

"Well," I said, "I never really thought about it. But sometimes the cars outside ..."

"Thicker curtains," he said. "Thicker curtains on your windows, or perhaps storm-windows. Then the noise wouldn't be so loud and you'd get better rest. You should also move your bed away from the window. That way you'll be in a more peaceful location."

"What's that got to do with my schoolwork?"

"Think about it," he said. "You don't sleep well; it's hard to get out of bed in the morning. It takes you a couple of hours to wake up properly, and by that time you've already daydreamed through a couple of classes."

"Wow!"

"Wow indeed," he said. He looked at the charts and then back at me. "Now look at this," he said, pointing around the hall. "Your front door is in the northeast part of your house. Do you know what that means?"

"Nope."

"It means that the crucial things in this family's fortune are knowledge and the life of the youngest son."

"Youngest son? But that's me!"

"Right. And this entrance hall is too cramped. All the good luck rushes in through the front door and it has nowhere to go, so it just sloshes around. Like you. If this hall were brighter, perhaps with a few mirrors, the luck would flourish, and so would the youngest son."

"I don't know what to say ..." I began.

"Another 'wow' will do fine," said the feng shui man.

"This is all a bit complicated," I said. "I need a snack."

"No, you don't," said the feng shui man, pointing at the blueprints. "You only think you do. That's because you can see the kitchen from the front door. Every time you stand in the hall, the first thought that enters your head is food. You're going to need to put a screen or a door *there*, or perhaps even some bookshelves *here*."

"Why?"

"Because then the first thing you'll think about when you walk in the front door will be reading. You know, getting on with your homework, studying for your tests, all that sort of thing."

"And you do this for a living?" I asked, dumbfounded.

"You bet," he said. "Once I've finished with this house, your luck situation is going to be cooler than a freezer in Greenland."

"And that's what you mean by changing the future?"

"That's right. Luck is just a word. There's no such thing as luck, really. You're doing badly at school at the moment because your window faces a busy road, your bed is too close to the window, you stub your toe on the doorstep every morning, and all kinds of things like that. You've also got a bedroom that encourages evil spirits and scares away good ones. We're going to change all that by moving a few things around. It's the simplest kind of magic spell, but one of the most effective."

"Did you say 'we'?" I asked.

"Oh, yes," he said. "Because I can tell you want to know more. Stick with me, kid, and you can become a feng shui master yourself."

"Stop calling me 'kid.'"

"I'll stop calling you 'kid,'" he said, "if you stop picking your nose."

"I wasn't picking my nose."

"Yes, you were. And it makes you look like a drooling idiot. No wonder your teachers think you're slow. You ever see grownups picking their nose?"

"Er, no."

"Why not?"

"Because only kids do it?"

"Right. So if you want grownups to treat you like a grownup...?"

"Er ... I shouldn't pick my nose."

"See?" said the feng shui man. "Easy. It's common sense. Just like feng shui."

"Oh."

"So let's get started," he said, turning back to the blueprints. And from that moment on, I wanted to be a feng shui master.

But it's tough being a feng shui master when, no matter how hard you protest, you're still basically a kid. You can't build your own home in a lucky location, so you have to live with whatever situation you find yourself in.

A lot of people don't believe in ghosts, or dragons, or evil spirits. They think that the supernatural world is nothing but superstition. But they don't know all the answers. They simply prefer not to ask all the difficult questions.

It's hard enough for adults to get everything in their home harmonious and charmed, so think how much more difficult it is for a youngster. Your parents wouldn't be too thrilled if you told them they had to demolish the garage to protect your home from evil spirits, or something like that. In fact, some people's parents wouldn't even let them hang lucky pictures in the right places to make sure that their house is charged with magical energy. But that's not a problem, because when you're young, your home isn't the house, because that was bought by someone else. When you're young, your home is your room. That's where you live and spend the most time, and that's where feng shui can bring the biggest amount of good fortune into your life.

This book will teach you how to do feng shui for yourself, to bring you a happier and more successful life. Once I started finding out about feng shui, I couldn't stop looking for more and more answers, asking more and more questions. I hope this book will start you on the same path towards good fortune and happiness. There are many ways to look at the world around us, but this can be one of the most exciting. And that's what I kept thinking as I listened to the feng shui man's stories ...

CHAPTER

2

Welcome to the Real World

The person who watches and learns from nature is a feng shui sorcerer. If you're the kind of person who enjoys puzzles, daydreaming, and stories, then you have the potential to be a magician too. Feng shui only looks like magic to people who don't think. It's as sensible as anything. The feng shui master looks, listens, and thinks. Then he or she comes up with a theory and tries it out. Eventually, the feng shui master discovers which methods work better than others and passes on the advice. Over the centuries, the advice of feng shui masters has been collected and passed on through family stories and old books. Back in the beginning, it all began with someone smart who thought faster and harder than the others. Someone like you.

Fast Food

How can feng shui affect your life? Surely luck is influenced by more than a few knickknacks? Yet you'd be surprised by how important your surroundings can be.

Let me tell you about a place that used to turn feng shui on its head. A well-known hamburger chain set up shop in Taiwan a few years ago. Their restaurants displayed very bad feng shui indeed, but it was all quite deliberate. Once people had paid money for their food, the company wanted them off the premises as fast as possible. So the lights were bright enough to glare off

the pages of your newspaper, the tables were so closely spaced that other people's conversations disturbed you, the seats would hurt your behind after about 20 minutes, and the background music was on a tapeloop, which was fine the first time, but annoying when you heard all the same songs again.

People who chose to eat in the restaurant didn't realize it, but they were being encouraged to finish their food quickly, so they could clear out and make way for more customers. It wasn't the Chinese way at all, since the Chinese prefer to make their restaurants such nice places that the customer is encouraged to return again and again, staying for a long time, and spending more money. But the thought that had gone into the design was very similar to the thought that goes into feng shui.

The difference was that the restaurant was deliberately designed to make life difficult. Feng shui is designed to make life easier.

Questions, Questions

If feng shui laws are dumped on you without explanation, they look insane. But most of them are based on observation. Generations of feng shui masters come and go. Every time one of them notices another strange little thing about the world, they open another file. More and more people come to them with questions, and the feng shui masters' files get bigger and bigger.

The feng shui masters think and experiment. They are detectives, weathermen, priests, psychiatrists, doctors, and scientists, all rolled into one. The world turns and the seasons come and go. Night follows day, and spring follows winter. One day, someone asks a real doozy of a question and the feng shui masters have to do some serious thinking.

For instance, what happens when someone dies?

CHAPTER 3

The World Beyond

"Hang on," I said. "I'm not dead. What's this got to do with me?"

"Well," said the feng shui man. "How do you know you're alive?"

"I just am! Aren't I?"

"If you say so," said the feng shui man. "But I was talking to your great-grandmother this morning, and she said —"

"You did what!? You can't talk to her! She died before I was born!"

"I know," he said. "Doesn't mean I can't ask her what she thinks of your exam results."

"But she's dead!"

"How do you know?"

"Well ... I ... er ..."

"You just do?" suggested the feng shui man. It seemed like the obvious answer, but I was quickly learning that feng shui masters aren't happy with obvious answers.

"She's still there," he said. "Just as real as you and me."

The Breath of Life

What is the difference between a living thing and a dead one? Something is missing. The feng shui masters' answer to this question is that the missing component is breath, or "qi" as it is called in Chinese. (Pronounce it "chee," to rhyme with "tea.") When something dies, the breath leaves its body and goes somewhere else. But qi is not merely the air that we breathe, it is also that essential part of you and me that makes us You and Me. In other words, it is our soul.

But we are not the only things that possess qi. Qi is a kind of energy that exists in everything. Like food, it can go off and turn bad. Feng shui is the science that helps you to keep your life full of good qi, and helps you to ward off bad qi that has gone stale.

Qi is all around us. Good qi is the happy glow you feel on a warm sunny day, the sound of children playing outside, birds singing in the trees, your favorite song or food or drink. It is a picture or a gift

that you are really proud of. It is that essential *something* about these things that makes them so good for you. It links you to events in nature, and to other people. Isn't it better to have others' approval rather than their anger? If people are happy with you, you are happier with yourself.

Bad qi is that miserable mood you're in when you have to walk home through the rain. It's the people next door playing their stereo too loud when you're trying to sleep. It's that certain *something* that makes you feel horrible when you're ill, instead of being able to enjoy lazing around in bed all day. It's that terrible fear you get inside when you know that you've done something wrong and it's only a matter of time before someone finds out.

But here's the good news. Qi can be controlled. You can live your life so that good qi rolls towards you all the time, and bad qi keeps away. That is what feng shui is all about. It's about encouraging the good things in life so that it keeps on getting better.

Qi is the breath of the universe. When you're full of energy for no reason you can think of, you have stumbled into a patch of good qi. And when you feel horrible, you're having a bad qi day.

THE STORY SO FAR

●✦ There is a magical energy called qi.

●✦ Qi can be good or bad.

●✦ We are surrounded by qi and can encourage the good to stay and the bad to go.

FOOD FOR THOUGHT: YOUR ENVIRONMENT

How do you feel right now? Are you tired or brimming with energy? Can you think of any reason why you might feel this way? Think about the place you're in right now while reading this book. How has the environment affected you? Perhaps you're trying to read this on a crowded bus, while all around you children are snapping rubber bands at each other, annoying the driver, and pestering each other for candy. Meanwhile, the bus is lurching back and forth, cars are zooming past, and the noise of everybody around you is making it hard to concentrate. How could the situation improve?

Or perhaps you're reading this book in the park, sitting with your back against a tree trunk. But what if the shadows of the branches keep on whizzing across the page and distracting you? What if the sun is too bright, or the grass is damp?

It would be nicer to be reading this book at home, with just the right amount of light—not too much so that it shines off the pages and hurts your eyes, and not so little so that you have to squint to see these words. How are you sitting? Are you hunched over the book or are you leaning back in a nice, comfy chair? Maybe, like me, you have the annoying habit of leaning back in your chair so that the front two legs lift off the floor. Is this a good idea, or do you suspect that you're so busy trying to balance that you're not concentrating on reading?

Wherever you are at the moment, take a minute or two to consider all the things that are going on around you. Use your senses, and think about how you could make the situation easier. How are you sitting? What can you hear? What can you smell? Can you see the page properly? Are you being distracted by hunger or thirst? Is the radio too loud? And if any of these turn out to be bad influences, what can you do to change them?

FOOD FOR THOUGHT: A CUP OF QI

Stop reading for a moment and have a glass of water. It doesn't have to be water, you can have any drink you like. Yum, lovely. That's because the fresh drink is charged with good qi. Now fill up the glass again but don't drink it. Leave it somewhere safe and make sure no one touches it. Leave it, if you can, for a few days. Feel like drinking it now? Of course not. There is dust and dirt in it. If you drink a glass of stale water, it tastes horrible. But what has changed? Water doesn't go off. No one has added anything to the water, or taken anything away. Nothing should have changed, but something has. The difference is qi. Qi flourishes in swirling, fresh water, but slowly fades away if the water is still. And, remember, qi exists in everything. This is why fresh air is so bracing but your attic or basement always smells musty and dusty. This is why exercise makes you feel good but lazy people always moan that they can't be bothered to do anything. Feng shui is the art of making sure that you and your luck remain like a cool, clear glass of water, as fresh as a daisy. Feng shui is the art of making sure that you, and your luck, never go stale. Qi behaves in a very similar way to water. The difference between good and bad qi is just like the difference between a clear, bubbling brook of fresh water and a smelly, stagnant swamp.

Creatures from Beyond

If there were special qi-goggles you could wear like X-ray glasses, you would see whirling lines of good qi joining you to the people you love. If you were wearing the qi-goggles when you were in a bad mood, you would see spiky lines of bad qi jabbing into people's heads and keeping them angry. You would also see ghosts.

Spirit creatures are also part of the natural world. However, they are incredibly hard to see because they don't have physical bodies. They are made from qi and nothing else. Just like people, some are good and some are bad. A lot of them couldn't care less and simply want to get on with their business. If a spirit becomes angry with you for some reason, it might haunt you as a ghost, or make your life a misery by hanging around while bad qi floats away from it and toward you. It can bring you bad luck.

If a spirit likes you, it might help you out. If you are surrounded by happy spirits, they will protect you from disaster. They will act like magnets for good qi, drawing luck into your life and making you feel positive about everything. Good spirits are all around us, and very helpful in bringing us luck. They are either kind, otherworldly beings, or more often the spirits of your ancestors, who want to look after you. The answer to where people go when they die is very simple to a feng shui master. They don't go anywhere. They're still here with us. They leave their bodies behind but their souls are made of qi, so they never die.

We can't see their world but it exists all around us. People go into the world beyond and carry on with their lives as they did before.

They still have old scores to settle. They still want those belongings that people borrowed and never returned. They still have the same hobbies and the same strange little quirks. They like to go back to their favorite places and visit their friends. My grandfather still likes to putter around his vegetable garden checking on the plants. I can't see him, but sometimes I can feel that he's there. Your ancestors are exactly the same. They still worry and fret about you, and check to make sure you're wrapped up warm and eating properly. This might sound weird at first, but to the feng shui master it sounds perfectly reasonable. Because love can survive anything, and that includes death.

Family Ties

They might be sitting next to you now, or they might have died centuries ago, but your ancestors still want to know how you are doing. They care about you, and you should care about them. No one exists in isolation; we all have a responsibility to follow orders from our elders and to help out those who are younger. If

you are a child in a big Chinese family, you must do everything that your parents and older relatives tell you, and they must do everything they can to help you on your way through life. You in turn are responsible for your younger siblings, and they must defer to you.

This is one of the golden rules of the Chinese world, but it's one that people like to ignore. Everybody loves the fairytales and fantastic legends of feng shui, and many devour feng shui books hoping to bring luck into their lives. But they ignore one of the most important aspects of feng shui. If you want Chinese luck, you must act in a Chinese way. And that means that you must listen to the advice of your seniors (parents, grandparents, uncles, aunts, teachers, etc.) and help your juniors (your younger brothers and sisters, cousins, nephews, nieces, and so on).

The Chinese afterlife is a lot like the world we live in. People live in towns, they have jobs, there are always things to do and people to see. Chinese people on Earth burn paper models of everyday objects so that the essence of these objects is sent to their ancestors in the world beyond. So if they think their ancestors need a new car in the afterlife, they don't have to send them a car. Instead, they burn a miniature paper car. That is enough qi to make a real car for their ancestors. They burn fake money, so that their ancestors beyond have plenty to spend. They burn paper houses, so their ancestors have somewhere nice to live. These days, they even burn paper fax machines, credit cards, and games consoles!

Luckily for most of us, we don't have to bother with such a dangerous form of magic. The eldest members of your family will already be looking after your ancestors in the spirit world, so you don't have to. They have pictures of your relatives so that your relatives are still part of family occasions. They put flowers on their graves so your relatives know that you still care about them, and they have a very sophisticated way of burning money called "tax," where they send money to the government, which then burns it for them in safety.

And, of course, as long as you're including your ancestors in your prayers and looking out for them, they'll be doing the same for you. People in the spirit world might not have fax machines, but they are friendly with all sorts of creatures that can help you out. They can put in a good word with the weather dragons so that your barbecue doesn't get rained off, they can ask spirit scholars to help you with your homework, and they can even have a quiet word with a few guardian angels, to make sure that you don't have an accident on your way home from school. In China, family obligations are a two-way street, even beyond the grave.

High Spirits

But your ancestors are not the only form of spirit. There are also immortals, who were powerful individuals in this world and who watch over everyone from their neighborhood. These spirits act like patron saints, even if they're not your ancestors, because if someone becomes famous their luck and success will rub off on everyone in their community.

For example, where I come from in Taiwan there was a very famous historical figure called Coxinga. He began life as a pirate, but when China was invaded by the Manchus 300 years ago the Emperor needed a fleet of ships. Unfortunately for him, he didn't have any, but Coxinga had hundreds of warships and trading vessels under his command. So the Emperor sent for Coxinga the Pirate King and made him an admiral.

Coxinga and his men fought bravely, but the Chinese armies were defeated on land and things looked hopeless. The old Emperor fled the country, and the Manchu barbarians became the new rulers of China. Coxinga retreated to his island base and the Manchus invaded the island to arrest him. That's how Taiwan first became part of China, but the spirit of Coxinga became the local guardian spirit of the island.

Three hundred years later, the Manchu dynasty had fallen and China was a republic. There was a revolution and the republicans had to flee the country with all their followers. They went to Taiwan, where the guardian spirit of Coxinga watched over them. China's new rulers always threatened to invade Taiwan and seize it back, but to this day they haven't got around to it. Feng shui masters say that this is because although Coxinga could not hold the island while he was a human being, now that he is a powerful spirit he has stronger magical powers, and is determined to protect his island from invaders.

THE STORY SO FAR

◆✦ We are surrounded by good and bad spirits made of qi. These are what we normally call "ghosts."

◆✦ Good ghosts, like your ancestors and local guardians, are your friends and will watch over you.

◆✦ You can make them feel welcome by putting pictures or mementos of them in your home.

◆✦ Spirits expect you to behave in the correct manner, and that means being kind to others.

◆✦ Famous people become immortals and watch over their entire community.

FOOD FOR THOUGHT: GUARDIAN ANGELS

Just as Taiwan is protected by the ghost of Coxinga, you might find that your neighborhood is protected by another famous person. Are there any famous people from your area? Check the libraries or the newspapers and see if you can find out anything about your local history. Your town may have produced a politician or a rock star, a sports giant or a famous soldier. Their ghosts will watch over the area, and their luck can rub off on you, especially if you have a picture or memento of them in the right part of your house. What about your relatives? Who do you think is watching over you right now? Do you know who your ancestors are, and what they were like?

Stuff about Dragons

"All right," I said. "Assuming this is all true, it still doesn't seem to have that much to do with feng shui. All you're saying is I should be nice to people."

"Well," he said, "that's a start, isn't it? Spirits aren't stupid. You can't *pretend* to be nice to people, you have to really do it. If you show respect to the spirits, they will reward you."

I didn't want to hear this; it was all sounding too much like hard work.

"Look," I said. "I didn't think feng shui was about ghosts and spirits and all that stuff. I thought it was about moving things around your home to change your fate."

"It is," said the feng shui man. "But the reason we move things around is to gather up the most powerful kind of qi, from the most powerful kind of supernatural creature."

"Which is what?"

"A dragon."

"Silly me, I should have thought of that."

"You don't sound convinced," he said.

Barbarians from the West like to describe dragons as nasty and dangerous creatures that breathe fire and fight knights in armor. There's no denying that dragons can breathe fire and are very dangerous, but there's more to Chinese dragons than that.

We like dragons. They are powerful creatures, but they are also very old and wise. And you don't get to be old and wise by being nasty and spiteful, so Chinese dragons are extremely kind.

The chances of you seeing one are quite remote, because even though they can appear in the real world they can also change shape. When dragons appear in their true form, people tend to panic and launch fighter aircraft because they think aliens are invading, which isn't very productive. Dragons like things to be peaceful and don't want to scare people, so they often travel in disguise. Most like to change into human form, but some pretend to be animals or birds. However, you must know what a dragon looks like because there are pictures of them all over the place, especially if you live near a Chinese restaurant or temple.

Just in case you do run into a dragon on your travels, remember to be polite. Dragons wield incredible power and should always be treated with respect and courtesy. Sometimes they like to test people to find out if they have good manners and souls, so watch out for the odd sneaky dragon trick. One of their favorites is to disguise themselves as human beings, to see if you are naturally kind to others or simply kind to large dragons out of fear. Shou Lao, the god of immortality, is particularly good at this. He likes to disguise himself as an old man to see if people will offer him their seat on the bus. If they do, he grants them luck.

In the unlikely event that you actually find yourself face to face with an undisguised dragon, take a look at its claws. Most dragons have three or four claws, but the oldest and most powerful have five. This is because, as imperial dragons, they have to read a lot of books and write a lot of letters, which is very difficult if you haven't got any thumbs.

Not even feng shui masters can agree on where dragons come from. One old story grows out of the fact that the dragon is China's guardian animal. Until the early years of this century, the Chinese flag had a huge dragon on it, and the Emperor sat on the Dragon Throne. The words for Emperor and dragon were sometimes interchangeable. Some feng shui masters suggest that, in olden days, the area we call China was made up of many different tribes, each with a different animal on its flag. As the tribes made alliances and conquered each other, they would combine their totem animals, and everything eventually got mixed up.

One day, the tribespeople found themselves with a really weird-looking animal on their flag. It had the horns of a deer, the head of a tiger, the body of a snake, the claws of a lion, the strength of

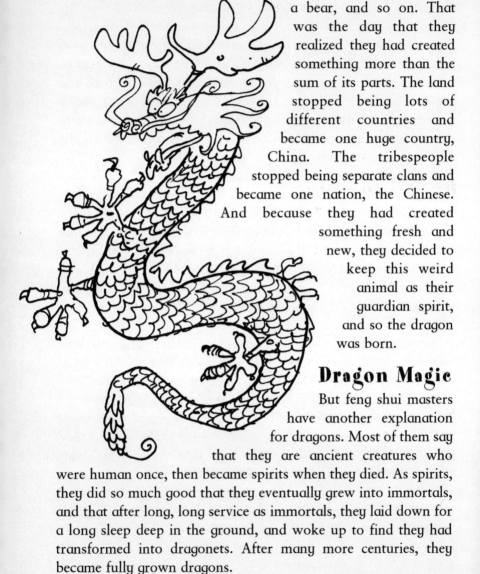

a bear, and so on. That was the day that they realized they had created something more than the sum of its parts. The land stopped being lots of different countries and became one huge country, China. The tribespeople stopped being separate clans and became one nation, the Chinese. And because they had created something fresh and new, they decided to keep this weird animal as their guardian spirit, and so the dragon was born.

Dragon Magic

But feng shui masters have another explanation for dragons. Most of them say that they are ancient creatures who were human once, then became spirits when they died. As spirits, they did so much good that they eventually grew into immortals, and that after long, long service as immortals, they laid down for a long sleep deep in the ground, and woke up to find they had transformed into dragonets. After many more centuries, they became fully grown dragons.

This story was used by feng shui masters to explain rather a lot.

They thought that earthquakes were caused by baby dragons springing free from the earth and taking their first flight. Young dragons were always rather feisty and used to play games with each other in the sky, which unfortunately resulted in massive thunderstorms and great big arcs of lightning. If you found yourself in a really big storm, chances were that dragons were in the sky fighting a battle with evil spirits. So it's best not to moan about the rain; life would be a lot worse if the dragons weren't up there looking after you.

Do Not Disturb

Dragons are so old that they need a lot of beauty sleep, and some of them sleep for many centuries. Sometimes they sleep for so long that everyone forgets they are there. But a snoring dragon puts out vast amounts of good qi. This flows from the dragon's snout in long lines of energy called dragonlines.

This is perhaps one of the major differences between East and West. Some barbarian sorcerers talk of lines of magical energy called leylines, and you might be forgiven for thinking that dragonlines are the same thing. But leylines are straight, whereas dragonlines like to meander and twirl around. Bad qi travels in straight lines because it's always in a rush to do more mischief, but good qi likes to take its time and smell the flowers along the way. The upshot of this is that bad luck tends to zip in and out of your life; whereas, when it eventually turns up, good luck can be enticed into hanging around for a long, long time.

Much of feng shui lore revolves around the location of kindly sleeping dragons, and with tracing the lucky dragonlines. A house protected by a dragon and surrounded by good qi will have healthy, lucky, successful occupants. Once you can gain access to the good qi that flows from nearby dragons, you are on the path to becoming an expert in do-it-yourself feng shui.

THE STORY SO FAR

◆✦ Dragons are powerful supernatural creatures.

◆✦ No one would dare to argue with a dragon, but sometimes dragons like to travel in disguise to see if the people they meet are kindhearted.

◆✦ Dragons are brimming with good qi, and it rubs off on people they meet.

◆✦ Good qi also comes from sleeping dragons, who are often buried beneath the earth. There may be one under your house, for all you know.

◆✦ The longer you spend in the presence of a dragon, the more qi rubs off on you.

◆✦ Good qi travels in long, slow curves.

◆✦ Bad qi travels in straight lines.

FOOD FOR THOUGHT: DRAGON SPOTTING

Seen any dragons lately? Probably not. But can you think of anywhere nearby where a dragon might be sleeping? A pretty lake, a grove of trees, or a big hill somewhere near your house? If you can see it from your window, the chances are that the good qi is rolling gently toward you at this very moment. If a place is naturally beautiful, it has a lot of good qi, and that means you're in luck. If you haven't got any pretty views from your windows, make your own with pictures on the walls. It's as easy as that.

Qi and the Natural World

"So where do I find dragons? I suppose I just hang around being nice to people," I said.

"You haven't been listening," said the feng shui man, calmly. "I just told you that dragons can appear in disguise as people."

"Right."

"But I also said that dragons can be forces of nature."

"So?"

"So the closer you are to the natural world, the more likely you are to be wrapped in a dragon's energy."

"Yeah, right," I said. "So what do I do? Look after the back yard and bring plants inside the house or something stupid like that?"

"Now," said the feng shui man, "I think you're finally starting to understand."

Feng shui was originally thought up for people who lived in the Chinese countryside, before the days of straight roads and noisy cars, and it still works best if you live somewhere quiet and peaceful. Even if you live in the middle of a busy city, peace and quiet within your home are very important for manufacturing and encouraging good qi. Look for patches of vegetation or trees that seem to be flourishing better than the areas around them. These places of luxuriant growth are evidence of good qi in the neighborhood, because their closeness to a dragon's breath gives them more power to grow. If you have potted plants around your house, you may notice that some of them do better than others. There may be a place in the house where the plants grow freely, and somewhere else where, no matter how hard you water them and no matter how carefully you look after them, they always seem to wither.

Feng Shui Outdoors

For many people who live in cities, the closest you get to country life is puttering about in the back yard, and if you have a small area of countryside like this behind your house you should treat it as an important asset for getting good qi.

In feng shui lore, your back yard is a small kingdom, and the way it is treated will show what kind of "royal family" rules over it. If the kingdom is in disarray, it may bring bad luck upon the royal family, so make sure that your back yard isn't too much of a mess.

A Walk in the Park

Another place where even city dwellers can see the feng shui of the countryside at work is in their local park. Many parks have winding paths that encourage people (and, of course, kindly spirits and good qi) to take their time and linger. Groundskeepers like gentle little hills, bubbling streams, fish ponds, and flowerbeds, because all these things help to turn the park into a reservoir of good qi, which is why these people can sometimes seem overly protective of their domain.

It is well known to feng shui masters (and groundskeepers) that evil spirits are liable to be woken up by newly tilled ground, which is why building sites are often off-limits and why groundskeepers get so annoyed about children riding their bicycles on the grass. Bicycles in parks are particularly bad news if you're a groundskeeper and part-time sorcerer, because you'll have spent many months carefully crafting gently winding paths and well-kept lawns, only to have a load of kids plow straight, demon-friendly trenches right across the middle with their tires. Respect your local park's cultivation of qi, and keep your wheels where they belong.

Natural Charms

Many centuries of feng shui study in the countryside left sorcerers with a list of natural things that seemed to bring in lots of good qi and to work as lucky charms.

Greenery is the most important lucky charm given to us by the natural world. Trees, flowers, plants, and shrubbery all help to harmonize the feng shui of your surroundings. For a start, caring for a plant will make you a kinder person. The sharp edges and unpleasant views that cause bad qi can be masked by well-placed potted plants, windowboxes, or trees planted in your back yard. Even Western barbarians are aware of this, because they rightly prefer hedges to fences, enjoy taking care of their back yards, and like having flowers and plants indoors. During the winter months, Western barbarians bring a tree into their house and decorate it with bright, lucky objects such as tinsel and ornaments. At a time of year when the world outside is barren and bleak, the indoor tree helps to bring nature into the lives of the barbarian family, and to bring them luck and growth in the year to come.

Another important natural force is water. Of course, if you have plenty of greenery in your dwelling, you'll need to water the plants and that will bring you even more luck. But people all over the world like a fish pond in their back yard or an aquarium in their living room. The water helps to prevent the room's atmosphere from becoming too dry, and the sound of bubbling water brings soothing qi to all who hear it.

The Chinese are particularly keen on goldfish, and many Chinese homes and restaurants have goldfish tanks in them. This is because when a goldfish passes through the gates of heaven it transforms into a dragon, and it may return as a dragon to help out the people who looked after it so well when it was a humble fish. Do bear in mind that goldfish will only work as feng shui charms if they are treated well. Don't keep pets if you're not going to look after them properly, otherwise you'll have to deal with an angry dragon and I wouldn't bet on you winning that particular fight.

THE STORY SO FAR

- Qi flourishes in the natural world, so the more natural your environment, the more qi you can generate.

- Green, growing things and bubbling water are important reservoirs of qi, not only outdoors in the countryside but also indoors in your home.

- And remember, you don't need to grow a huge tree in your bedroom. In fact, you don't need to grow anything. Feng shui operates just as well with pictures or representations of beautiful things as it does with the objects themselves.

FOOD FOR THOUGHT: NATURE IN YOUR HOUSE

Take a good, long look at your room. Is plenty of natural light coming in through the windows? Do you have a nice view of nature through the windows? Do you have any plants to care for and brighten the room? Or do you have any pictures of plants or trees or scenes of natural beauty? Is there anything about your room that really bugs you? If it does, is there anything you can do to change it?

FOOD FOR THOUGHT: NATURE OUTDOORS

What's the difference between walking down a crowded street and walking through a quiet, pretty park? Do you feel different in each place? Ask yourself what the difference is between the two places, and try to think of ways to bring those differences into your life. Use your senses again, and try to identify the things that make the park a better place to be in than the crowded street.

CHAPTER

6

Feng Shui at Home

"With me so far?" asked the feng shui man.

"Kind of," I said. "Except this is all pretty useless."

"Why?"

"Because if I did everything you said, I'd end up living in a shed in the back yard or a treehouse or somewhere like that, and that won't make me lucky, it'll just make me stupid."

"Oh."

"Yeah! Come on, think about it. I'm not going to trade in a nice warm house just so I can 'get closer to nature.' I'm not going to rip up the floorboards and plant trees in the living room, either."

"Finished?"

"Er, yes …"

"Because," said the feng shui man, "I haven't even started yet."

You spend the largest amount of time inside your house, and so the internal feng shui of your home is very important.

In the modern world, people are unlikely to build their own

houses, which makes it difficult for a new convert to feng shui to plan ahead properly. You will often find yourself having to compromise, to live with other people's magical mistakes, and sometimes in the shadow of other people's bad qi. It's not only the bad qi itself that you have to worry about, you'll also have to be on the lookout for evil spirits made of, or feeding on, all the bad qi around you. Cities are crawling with good and bad spirits, and you will want to encourage the first kind and scare off the second.

Raising the Roof

You may have noticed that a lot of buildings in the Far East have curvy roofs shaped a bit like ski jumps. The shape is no coincidence; if demons fall out of the sky on to your house, they will normally slide down the roof and end up in your back yard. If your back yard has a wall around it, the only way back out again is by traveling through your house and, who knows, they might even decide to stay and never leave. A curvy roof avoids this problem. The demons fall out of the sky, roll down the roof as normal, and then go flying off the end and out into the big wide world. Hey presto, you're safe, although your neighbors might get annoyed because this increases the chance of evil spirits landing in their own back yards.

If, by some accident, you find yourself living near a building with a curvy roof pointing straight at you, there's a small chance that demons bouncing off it will end up somewhere near your house. If this is the case, make sure that you have no windows facing it. If you do have windows facing the demons' ski jump, you'll need to put something reflective on the other side of the room, so that if the demons do come charging into your house, they will bounce back out again.

Mirror, Mirror

No one knows exactly why demons are so scared of mirrors, but these simple devices have done the trick since ancient times. When mirrors were first invented (about 3,000 years ago, by the best estimates) they were people's first chance to see what they really looked like. The feng shui masters explained that when you looked in the mirror you weren't looking at the real world because everything was reversed. What you actually saw was your soul.

Later on in history, people in Hong

Kong started to tell another story about mirrors and demons. Demons are not pleasant creatures to look at. In fact, the average demon has a face like a box full of frogs. They're as ugly as anything but have never seen their own reflections because there aren't any mirrors in hell. So imagine what happens when a really ugly demon comes charging into your house looking for the chance to do some mischief. He—or possibly she, since some of the worst demons are girls—will land on the roof, swing down and through an open door or window, run up the stairs looking for a fight, and then bump straight into a mirror. But then the demon gets an eyeful of just how ugly it really is, and then he, or she, will scream in terror and go charging straight out again. An excellent result!

Me and My Shadow

To see how useful mirrors are for scaring demons, just imagine how handy they are against earthly invaders. Have you ever been spooked by your own reflection? You'll be walking down the street and you suddenly think there's someone next to you, only to discover that it's your own reflection in a store window. Now imagine that you're a thief breaking into someone's house. You're all fired up and nervous, worried that you might get caught, so the

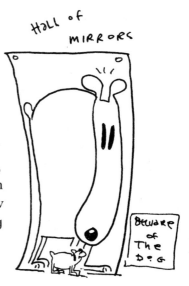

last thing you want to happen is to be frightened by the thought that there might be someone else in the house. Suddenly, out of the corner of your eye you see a figure moving, and you panic and run for it. The house is saved, you've been thwarted, and all because of a mirror cunningly placed near the front door.

Mirrors in Feng Shui

Mirrors are particularly useful in a variety of settings. They can be placed opposite badly situated doors to bounce evil spirits back to where they came from. They can also be used to counter the bad qi of an irregular-shaped room. If your room has a jutting corner, the sharp point will work like a knife to stab bad qi into the middle of your house. But a mirror on the corner will create the illusion of more space, and dispel the problem. Mirrors are also particularly useful in shadowy areas (such as rooms with small windows) because they double the amount of light by reflecting it back into the room. If you have a room that doesn't get much sunlight, you can increase its airiness by putting a large mirror on the wall opposite the window. This will bounce what little light there is back into the room, making it much more qi-friendly.

Many shopkeepers, even among the Western barbarians, like to put huge mirrors along their walls. By reflecting the rest of the shop back at itself, these mirrors make it look twice as large and spacious, creating a less cramped feeling. A popular practice among Chinese shopkeepers involves putting a mirror near the cash register so they can symbolically "double" the amount of money they take. Look out for this next time you're in a Chinese restaurant.

Other kinds of mirror are used in feng shui, but I don't have the space to say too much about them here. One is the exorcist's mirror used by the most powerful feng shui masters to capture demons that refuse to budge. The feng shui master traps the demon within the mirror with a secret spell, then takes the mirror somewhere safe where it is broken and the pieces are scattered at the bottom of the ocean. This operation is as dangerous as it sounds but, luckily for you, you won't have to worry about it if your house already has good feng shui.

Ground Lovers

Some demons run along the ground, as opposed to dropping in from the sky. Demons, like bad qi, are very bad at turning corners, which is good news if you live on a bendy street or have a curvy path leading up to your house. Demons are also notoriously bad at climbing steps because, frankly, they're a bit stupid. If you ever go to a Chinese temple, you may notice that there is a large block lying across the entrance, not unlike a "speed bump."

Nowadays we use speed bumps in the road to slow down cars in quiet neighborhoods, but before that they were used to make life difficult for demons. Your average demon, you see, is so intent on causing trouble that he (or she) can only hop over two steps at a time. Put an odd number of steps in front of him, and he's flummoxed. Build a single, big step and he'll waste all day trying to bounce over it. With a larger, odd number of steps he'll get all the way up to the last step, and then spend hours trying to

work out how to get over it. So if your house can only be reached by traveling up steps, you'll be completely safe as long as there's an odd number of them. If there's an even number, you still run the risk of demon invasion, but once you've read this book you will be more than capable of scaring them off, even if they get inside the building.

Taking the Right Steps

It is considered bad feng shui to have a front door that opens directly on to a straight staircase, because this means that the good qi from upstairs can zoom right out of the house, while bad qi and demons can come charging in from outside. If your house fits this description, bounce the bad vibes back with a mirror facing the door.

Picture Perfect

Another excellent way of increasing the good qi in your house is through the use of paintings, posters, pictures, and other objects. Just as Western barbarians hang pictures on their walls to brighten up the room, Chinese people use pictures to help their feng shui. You can offset the bad qi in unlucky sectors of your house by placing representations of guardian spirits there. This is why some Chinese buildings have statues of dogs or lions outside, to protect the occupants by scaring away evil spirits.

3It will help to bring you good luck if you place a statue of a saint, or a picture of something with good qi, in an unlucky area. Holy books, such as the Bible or Koran, are particularly effective in scaring spirits away. You can use the same tactic to encourage good spirits. How about keeping your schoolbooks in the knowledge sector of your house (see Chapter Seven)? You might find that they attract kind spirits who make your homework easier.

Pennies From Heaven

Many Chinese homes use coins as a means of protection, and also as a way to bring money into the lives of the occupants. The Chinese like to string a number of coins (normally five) on a length of red silken thread and hang them on the wall or by the window. But to do this you'll need a particular type of coin which is very uncommon. The best kind to use is an old-fashioned Chinese one, which is round with a square hole in the middle. Obviously, these are rather hard to find, and often expensive. But don't despair, because in feng shui you can use the element itself to represent particular items. Coins are metal, so any metal object will work equally well.

Instead of wasting your time (and money) hunting around antique shops or sending people off to China, why not use round scraps of aluminum foil or bottle caps? These are much easier to find and pierce, and will work just as well to make you richer. Anything metallic and shiny will do; it's all made from the same element, after all.

For Whom the Bell Tolls

Another popular metal object is the bell or wind chime. When bells ring they open a gateway to heaven, which is why you find bells in both Chinese temples and Western churches. Wind chimes are even better, but are best kept somewhere near the wind! Just outside the door or window is the best place for them. This is because wind chimes have a double purpose in feng shui. During the day their gentle music welcomes good spirits and scares away demons, but at night when all is quiet they act as temporary resting places for wandering ghosts. These spirits have nowhere else to go, either because they have no descendants left to look after them any more or because they are demons.

A wind chime provides the wandering spirits with somewhere to stay for the night, which cheers them up and makes them less likely to blow down the walls of your house. It also holds them at arm's length outside, which might distract them from coming in and causing any trouble. And it increases the chances that a lonely ghost with no descendants might adopt you and stay around to bring you luck.

Almost anything else can be used as a magic charm, which is a fact that even Western barbarians have understood over the centuries. Why else do people wear T-shirts decorated with their favorite pictures or people? Why else do families put nice ornaments in rooms or paint things in their favorite colors? If you like it and it makes you feel good, it's a charm that can be used to bring you good qi. If it's something scary, or something that makes you feel uneasy, then the chances are that it's got bad feng shui and shouldn't be anywhere near you.

THE STORY SO FAR

●✦ Demons are made of, and feed on, bad qi.

●✦ If your home is calm and peaceful, everything will be fine.
But in a big city, you have to watch out for the evil
spirits attracted by other people's bad qi.

●✦ Demons are scared of mirrors and
have trouble getting over steps.

●✦ Demons run in straight lines, so are
easily warded off by curves.

●✦ You can encourage things to happen by "reminding"
yourself of them – for example, you can increase your
wealth by surrounding yourself with bright metal objects.

●✦ If you have a picture or model of something in your home,
it is as good as having the real thing there.

FOOD FOR THOUGHT: "REMINDING" FENG SHUI

We've already mentioned that the sight of books encourages someone
to read. The feng shui man also pointed out that the sight of the kitchen
or food is more likely to make you hungry. Some might call that feng
shui, and others might argue that it's plain common sense.

Feng shui is all about making life easier for yourself, and the "magical"
parts of it grow out of the simplest things. My mother always refuses to
go to the supermarket until after dinner, because she says if you go
shopping when you're hungry you always buy more food than you need.
The fact that she hasn't eaten "reminds" her that she needs to buy
food, so she ends up buying loads of it.

If you have a remote control, try watching television without it for an evening. You will probably find that you change channels less often, mainly because you can't be bothered to get up and switch them. Having the remote-control in your hand doesn't make the programs on television any more or less interesting, it simply makes it easier for you to flick between them. The remote-control just "reminds" you that it's possible to change channels.

Feng shui is all about "reminding" yourself that it's possible to be happy, rich, or successful. After a while, it becomes second nature.

The Magic Octagon

"But —" I began.

"But what?" asked the feng shui man.

"You've told me nothing! All you've said is that I should surround myself with things that I like, and get rid of things that I don't."

"So?"

"When you came here, you said that you could change the future."

"Ah yes …," said the feng shui man. "The good bit."

"How do I do it?"

"You have to know where to put things in your room for the maximum luck," he answered.

"And how do I know where to put them?"

"You will need," he said, "an octagon!"

"Sounds painful," I said.

"It's as easy as north and south," he said, which didn't make any sense at all. As usual.

For a long time, the rules of feng shui remained a kind of folklore and were ignored by everyone else. Everything changed about 2,000 years ago, when two powerful warriors were involved in a fierce battle and both used feng shui masters to help them.

The First Compass

The Qin Emperor was having a very bad day. No sooner had he become China's first ruler than he was challenged by the rebel prince Chi Yu. In the middle of the battle, Chi Yu's sorcerers summoned up a magical mist to hide all their soldiers. The Qin Emperor was in trouble, and he knew it. But the Emperor had magic of his own, a

sorcerer's magical stone that always pointed in the same direction. He led his troops right into the fog, following the direction indicated by his compass. The compass led him and his army towards Chi Yu's hiding troops, and the Emperor was victorious.

The compass was a very important discovery for the world but was put to different uses. In the barbarian West, it was used for navigation, sending ships all over the world. Although some Chinese sailors did use the compass to travel far and wide, China is such a big *inland* country that it spent much of its time looking inwards, not outwards to the ocean.

The Compass in Feng Shui

Yet the compass was used for feng shui, and it can be one of the most important tools. Chinese farmers had already noticed several important things about the way the universe worked. The sun rose in the east, traveled across the sky and set in the west. Because China is above the Equator, the warmest direction was to the south, which got more sunlight. The coldest direction was to the north, not only because it got less sunlight but because that was where the cold Siberian winds came from.

If we divide everything up into four main directions, north, south, east, and west, and four minor directions (northeast, southeast, southwest, and northwest), we get a magical, eight-sided picture called an octagon. Houses and the rooms within them are all subject to this octagon.

Each point of the compass rules a different area of your life. It also rules different parts of the body, different members of your family, and different colors. The magic octagon is the product of hundreds of years of observation and experimentation by Chinese feng shui masters. If it looks complicated, that's because it is, but don't panic, I'm going to show you how to use it.

NORTH

WEST

SOUTH

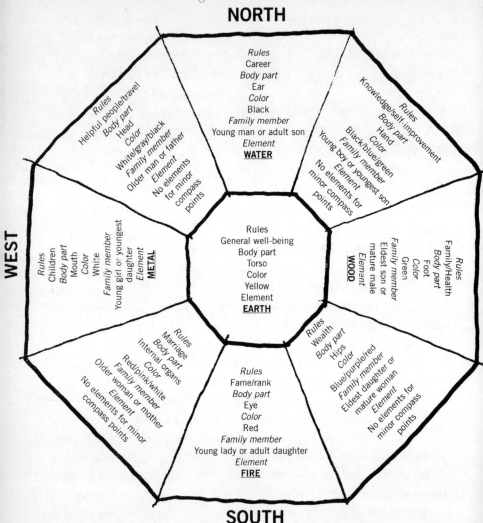

Rules
Career
Body part
Ear
Color
Black
Family member
Young man or adult son
Element
WATER

Rules
Helpful people/travel
Body part
Head
Color
White/gray/black
Family member
Older man or father
Element
No elements
for minor
compass
points

Rules
Knowledge/self-improvement
Body part
Hand
Color
Black/blue/green
Family member
Young boy or youngest son
Element
No elements for
minor compass
points

Rules
Children
Body part
Mouth
Color
White
Family member
Young girl or youngest daughter
Element
METAL

Rules
General well-being
Body part
Torso
Color
Yellow
Element
EARTH

Rules
Family/Health
Body part
Foot
Color
Green
Family member
Eldest son or
mature male
Element
WOOD

Rules
Marriage
Body part
Internal organs
Color
Red/pink/white
Family member
Older woman or mother
Element
No elements for minor
compass points

Rules
Fame/rank
Body part
Eye
Color
Red
Family member
Young lady or adult daughter
Element
FIRE

Rules
Wealth
Body part
Hips
Color
Blue/purple/red
Family member
Eldest daughter or
mature woman
Element
No elements for
minor compass
points

So how do you use the octagon? The octagon fits inside nations, buildings, rooms, and even single objects such as your bed or desk. First you need to work out which direction is north. There are several ways to do this.

1 Ask. Someone might know.
2 Work out where the sun rises and sets in relation to your house. Once you know where east and west are you can turn the octagon around until it points in the proper direction.

3 Get a compass and place it in the middle of the octagon. Turn the octagon underneath it until the needle on the compass points to the north sector of your octagon.
4 If you haven't got a compass you can make one. You will need a lodestone and a piece of string. Tie the string around the middle of the lodestone and hold it up. The bar will twist and turn and eventually come to rest with its north pole pointing north and its south pole pointing south. Make sure that you don't mix up north and south—it could be nasty.

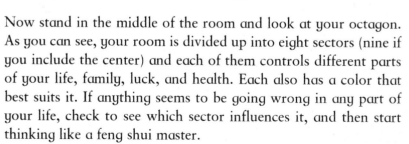

Now stand in the middle of the room and look at your octagon. As you can see, your room is divided up into eight sectors (nine if you include the center) and each of them controls different parts of your life, family, luck, and health. Each also has a color that best suits it. If anything seems to be going wrong in any part of your life, check to see which sector influences it, and then start thinking like a feng shui master.

For example, let's look at the north on the octagon. You will see that this direction is the ruler of your career. The part of the body it rules is the ear. Its element is water and its color is black. Young men or adult sons in the family are particularly favored by this direction. So if you're having trouble with your career, your ears, or any adult males in the family, then this is the part of the room or home that requires a little creative feng shui.

Are there any sharp corners throwing bad qi into that area? Are there any nasty influences such as drafts or unpleasant views? Is there too much shadow or too much light? Is the area too untidy? If none of these questions apply, it's time to start using magical items such as colors, charms, and pictures. (There will be more about this later on, so don't panic.)

Your Front Door

The front door is an important part of the house, and not only because you wouldn't be able to get in without it. It is the gateway to luck and your portal to the outside world. Whichever side of your house's magic octagon contains the front door will be a very strong influence on your life. If your door is in the north side of your house, then career will be of paramount importance. If your door is in the south side of your house then fame will be important, and so on. Normally, this is a good thing, and your door feng shui will bring you success in the related area. However, the feng shui of your door can also bring trouble if bad feng shui is involved, because the placement of your door will magnify it many times.

Let's imagine that your front door is in the eastern wall of your house. Your octagon will tell you that this emphasizes family and health, and also that this is the sector that rules the feet, and the fate of the family's eldest son or mature males. A family moving into a house like this is likely to be happy and healthy, likely to have more male children than female (who may be good at running). But ...!

Let's suppose there's a pillar just inside the door, or that the door opens into a tiny, cramped hall. Good qi rushes into the house but has nowhere to go. It splashes around the hall and is blocked. In such a house, expect the highlighted eastern sector to become a very unlucky, instead of lucky, area. The parents will

quarrel, everyone will be sick all the time, and the eldest son will be particularly badly affected. He is also likely to have smelly feet. Simple objects in the offending area can make all the difference. A mirror, for example, will make the hallway look bigger, and solve the problem instantly.

Another important consideration is what sort of room the front door opens into. The first thing you see when you open the front door will be the foremost thing in the feng shui and history of your house. If your front door opens in sight of a study or a living room, then your household life will be smart or happy. However, other rooms are less lucky. If the first thing you see is a bedroom, you will always be tired. If the first thing you see is a kitchen, you will always be hungry. If the first thing you see is a toilet, then you're really in trouble, and not just because you'll be spending more time than you'd like communing with the gods of the water closet. Toilets can flush away riches and good qi.

If your front door opens on to an unlucky area, the best thing to do is to wall it off symbolically with a mirror. You can also attempt to balance the bad luck by placing a lucky charm in the relevant part of the house's octagon.

Other Portals

Of course, doors are not the only ways into a house or room. Other entrances and exits have a weaker, but still noticeable, effect. This is why feng shui masters are so keen on the whereabouts of windows and suchlike. If a toilet is in plain sight, it will act as an escape chute for the qi of whatever sector it's in. Fireplaces also work like magical, secret doors. Why do you think Santa Claus comes down the chimney in all the stories? It's a way for spirits to sneak in and out of a house without anyone noticing. (And yes, of course there's a Santa Claus. The so-called Christmas "spirit" is a massive buildup of good qi in people's homes as the year comes to a close and we start to count our blessings and be nice to each other for once. You don't have to be a Christian to get a whiff of all that good qi pinging around in the atmosphere.)

Using Your Octagon

It's best to start with something you know, so let's pick a room in your house and try out the octagon. Stand facing north in the middle of the room and see what the octagon diagram has to say about your current living arrangements. Take each point of the compass in turn and check what is in each sector. Start with the structure of the walls themselves. Are they flat or curved, or does any sector have sharp, pointed corners shooting bad qi at you? If there are sharp corners pointing into a sector, can you think of a way that they might have badly affected your luck? What is on the wall? Perhaps we're looking at wallpaper, tiles, or bare bricks. Is the wall pleasing to the eye? If the colors are bright and stark, do they fit the color scheme for that part of the octagon? If the colors are muted and neutral, they won't affect the room's feng shui for better or worse, which is why many people prefer neutral colors on their walls. It is better to be safe than sorry, after all.

Are there any pictures on the wall? If so, what do they show? Now that we know which area of your life is ruled by this sector, do you think the subject of the picture brings good or bad qi into your life? Have you committed any obvious, major errors on your walls that immediately spring to mind? My sister, for example, gets involved in a lot of animal charity work, and she had a picture of a sad, lonely puppy on her wall. But the picture used to be in the southeast sector (wealth), dooming her and her chosen charities to be as wretched as the dog in the photograph. I told her to move it to the northwest (travel) sector. Just to be difficult, she ignored me and secretly moved it to the south (fame). Her fund-raising efforts around the school turned her into something of a local celebrity, which in turn brought in more money for her charity. To this day, she refuses to admit that feng shui had anything to do with her newfound success but, funnily enough, she's kept that picture in its new position.

Remember that, at the most basic level where feng shui is still more like common sense than magic, the pictures on your wall and the objects in your room function as reminders. Just as dogs tend to look like their owners, people often start to look like their houses. If the decoration in your house keeps on "reminding" you to be kind to others, or to work hard, or to take more holidays, some of it is bound to rub off on you.

At the more advanced level, where feng shui stops making obvious sense and we have to start taking the sorcerers' word for it, the sectors of the octagon are hidden influences on your luck and life. What furniture and objects are in that sector? At the back of this book is an alphabetical listing of some of the more common household objects and pictures, with explanations of their meaning in feng shui. But for now, let's concentrate on the most basic aspects. Is there anything sharp or pointed there? If so, it might be working like a thorn in your good qi. Is anything annoying there, such as a fragile object that you fret about knocking over? If so, have you ever considered moving it out of harm's way? And not just its harm, your harm as well! You could do without all that worrying, after all.

FOOD FOR THOUGHT: HELLO, STRANGER

Pretend for a moment that you are a stranger walking into the room. And you're not just any old stranger, either, you're a great detective. What can you see around the room? What does it tell you about the occupants? Are they clean or messy? Reliable or sloppy? Fun-loving or dull? Rich or poor? Happy or sad? Now, bearing in mind that this is your room, what would you like a stranger to think when he or she walked in? Don't imagine that I'm trying to encourage you to be the kind of shallow person who runs around leaving expensive magazines in plain view when someone comes to visit, in the vain hope that the visitor will be impressed. Instead, what I'm suggesting is that you start by trying to impress yourself. If you met yourself on the street, would you want to be friends with you? If not, why not? What's wrong with you? Why wouldn't you want to invite yourself round for dinner?

BASIC OCTAGON CHECKLIST

Room   What happens in this room? Who "belongs" to it (or rather, spends the most time here)? It is they who will be most affected by whatever goes on here.

Sector   Check the octagon to see what is ruled by this compass point.

Wall   Flat, curvy, or with sharp corners pointing bad qi at you? If you are facing sharp corners, can you soften them in some way?

Wall decoration   Bare brick, wallpaper, a pattern? Is there a picture on the wall?

Furniture and knickknacks   What objects are in this sector? Do you think they are affecting the qi in the room? If so, would they be better off somewhere else?

Elements and Colors

"Now this," I said, "could be useful."

"Oh," said the feng shui man. "Good."

"If only it made more sense," I added.

"What do you mean?"

"Well, I now know which part of the room affects what, and I'm starting to get an idea about moving stuff around, but I'm still not sure exactly what I should do to improve things."

"Like what?"

"That's it, like what? I still don't know. Let's imagine that I'm doing badly at school and want to sort out my bad qi."

"Okay."

"So, I know that knowledge and self-improvement are ruled by the northeast sector ..."

"Right."

"But I don't know how to change it, really. What am I supposed to put there? How do I know I won't make things worse if I start shifting things around? Which color goes where?

What shape is good and what shape is bad? I bet you're just about to tell me it's not the same for everyone, because otherwise everyone's houses would look exactly alike, wouldn't they? So how do I know what's right for me? I don't know how to get things equal, I don't know how to get everything, sort of, er ..."

"Balanced?" suggested the feng shui man, helpfully.

"Yes, balanced."

"That," said the feng shui man with a smile, "is the next bit."

Balancing Yin and Yang

The Chinese like things to be balanced. They like to look at the universe in terms of yin and yang, or rather dark and light. It's important that you don't confuse this with good and evil, because yin and yang aren't good or evil. They're just there.

You have probably seen the yin-yang symbol at some point in your life. It looks like two little tadpoles circling around each other. One is black and the other is white, but each has a tiny dot of the other in its center. They need each other. You can't have one or the other, you have to have both to make up the whole symbol, which is a sign that all is right with the world.

Night needs day, the sun needs the moon, light needs shade, husbands need wives, and vice versa. A beach without the sea isn't a beach, it's a desert, and this need for opposites is a fundamental part of the universe. The page you're looking at right now needs black and white. If the ink was white, you wouldn't see these words, and if the paper was black, you still wouldn't see them. You need yin and yang, otherwise the universe grinds to a halt and nothing gets done.

People, too, are yin and yang. But the Chinese idea of perfection is to have equal quantities of both. Yin things are dark, quiet, and peaceful. The night, the shade, and darkness are yin.

Yin is seen as a "female" component of the universe, so if you're a girl you'll already have a lot of yin in your character.

Yang areas are bright, loud, and boisterous. Day, light, and brightness are yang. Yang is seen as a "male" component of the universe, so if you're a boy you'll already have a lot of yang in your character.

Yin-yang Overdose

If you've got too much yang, you'll be completely hyperactive! You'll be rushing all over the place, yelling at the top of your voice. You'll always be outdoors, you'll always be too busy. Maybe you need to calm down a bit. You'll need more yin in your yang life.

If you've got too much yin, you might be too slow. You won't feel like going anywhere or doing anything: you'll be really quiet, or maybe you'll find that no matter how hard you try to make people listen to you, they'll always ignore what you're saying. You'll prefer to stay indoors, but you'll be bored with whatever is going on around

you. You'll need more yang in your yin life.

So how do you balance these parts of your life? We've already talked about the use of lucky charms, but there's another way which is even more powerful, and that's the use of the elements and the stars to choose lucky colors for you.

In feng shui, something as simple as the colors that surround you can bring you better qi. The colors around you might be the paint on your walls, the overall colors of the pictures, the clothes you wear, or even the color of your watchband, belt, or bracelet. Just imagine if all of the above were working in your favor to bring you more luck. You'd have more luck than you'd know what to do with!

There are five elements in Chinese thought – that is to say, five building blocks that go together to make up the universe. Everything (and everyone) is made up of differing amounts of these elements, and one of the jobs of a feng shui master is to make sure that the elements in your life are well balanced.

Fire

It was the discovery of fire that helped people to cook food, to make tools, and to scare away the creatures of the night. Before feng shui masters there were firemakers, who were regarded by primitive people as another kind of sorcerer, because they had the power to burn forests if they were in a bad mood, and to cook a nice dinner if they were happy. Fire's color is red, which is considered lucky by the Chinese. Chinese brides wear red on their wedding day, and Chinese people send each other red "good luck" cards on special occasions. The more Fire symbols you have in your life, the more dynamic, sparky, successful, and lucky you will be. But too much Fire in your life will exhaust you; you'll be too busy, you'll eat up everything in your path, and you might get out of control. Too much Fire might make you overconfident and self-absorbed. Fire is a yang element, so reds and Fire objects will bring more yang into your life.

Water

Water is another magical element to the Chinese, because in olden times it was the only way that you could see your reflection. The first mirrors were made by wiping a sheen of water across a flat, polished stone. Human beings can't live without water. In fact, you can exist without food longer than you can without water. In times of famine, thirst is even more dangerous than hunger. Much of the planet is covered by water. It is ancient and mysterious, like the sea that gave birth to us. Water's color is black, but sometimes blue. That's because the Chinese occasionally get confused between blue and green. They have 13 different kinds of red to choose from, but blue and green sometimes get mixed up. Between you and me, I think that spirits are smarter, and realize that water is blue, so you can get away with using blue if you want. But the ancient Chinese used black because that is the color of dark, unfathomable depths. Because water flows to fill whatever holds it, the more Water symbols you have in your life, the calmer, more sensitive, creative, and adaptable you will become. But too much Water in your life will make you easily hurt or indecisive. A bit wet, in other words.

Wood

This element not only represents the wood that makes desks, chairs, and paper, but also includes all plants and growing things. For this reason, the element of Wood is represented by the color green. There is something wonderful about the way things grow, about the way in which a seed placed in the ground will put out a shoot and roots, fight its way to the surface and grow into a plant, a bush, or even a huge tree. It takes such a long time for a tree to grow, but it does so slowly and surely. Walls can't resist the slow, relentless advance of a tree root. Tree roots can push up paving stones and roads. Trees represent all that is quiet and confident, all that is careful but ultimately victorious. Because trees and plants flourish and bloom in the right environment, the more Wood symbols you have in your life, the more understanding and helpful you will be to other people. But too much Wood will make you boring and impenetrable. If your tree grows too tall, it runs the risk of being struck by lightning. Also, watch out that too much Wood doesn't attract a carpenter who's looking for material. A tree that is too big runs the risk of being cut down, so too much Wood in your life may cause others to take you for granted and demand too much of your time.

Metal

These days we are surrounded by metallic objects, which makes it easy to forget how amazing they are. Metal actually comes from rocks in the ground, which you have to heat to incredible temperatures until the molten metal flows out like super-hot goop. Then you have to shape it and let it cool to form something incredibly hard and resilient. Metal makes swords and plows, bells and pen nibs. It also makes money, gold bars, and computers. The Metal element is very important in the modern world; as important as fire was to our ancestors. It is represented by the colors silver, gold, and white. But white should be used sparingly in clothing because it is also the Chinese color of mourning. Metal makes money, so the more Metal in your life, the richer you can be. But Metal also makes knives and swords, and too much Metal may make you unkind to others and obsessed with wealth.

Earth

Earth is the world, and where would we be without anything to stand on? Earth feeds the plants and animals, it gives us metals and fuels, it holds everything in its grasp. It is vast and all-encompassing. It makes bricks to build houses, it makes mountains and hills. It was here before us and will still be here long after we have gone. It is represented by all shades of brown, up to and including a dullish yellow. This is because there are parts of China where the earth actually is this color; it is the silt washed away from the riverbanks that give China's famous Yellow River its name. Earth is also a magical element to the Chinese because it includes sand, which gives us crystals and glass. Because Earth is at the foundation of everything, the more of it there is in your life, the steadier and more confident you will become. But too much Earth will make you pigheaded and stubborn, and liable to overextend yourself like a rocky overhang on a cliff. Take care that everything doesn't come tumbling down in a landslide.

FOOD FOR THOUGHT: WALKING THE TIGHTROPE

Remember that balance is everything with the elements. It is possible to have too much of a good thing. You can represent different elements in your room or in a weak sector by either placing examples of each element (a plant for Wood, for example, a goldfish bowl for Water, metal objects for Metal, and so on), pictures of such examples (a picture of something fiery for Fire), or even just the colors that rule each element. Suppose that you feel your qi is lacking in Metal. You could have metal objects around you, silvery things like mirrors, or white walls. All of this would contribute to your qi, bringing you into balance. As well as balancing your Metal deficiency, it might also bring you luck in money matters, because money is Metal.

Each element also has a particular kind of shape as its symbol—

curvy things for Water,

triangular things for Fire,

rectangular things for Wood,

trapezoid shapes for Earth,

and the other indescribable one
(just look at the picture, I don't know
what it's called!) for Metal. All of these
things can be used to balance the
elements in your life.

ELEMENT CHECKLIST

●✦ Feng shui states that five building blocks make up the universe. These are Fire, Water, Wood, Metal, and Earth.

●✦ Everything is made up of these elements. Even you.

●✦ But if you have too much or too little of a certain element, you will need to balance it.

●✦ You can do this by placing shapes, colors, or objects belonging to the other elements around your room.

CHAPTER 9

Elements and the Chinese Zodiac

"See?" asked the feng shui man. "Easy!"

"No it isn't," I said. "You've answered one question, but now you've left me with an even harder one."

"What do you mean?"

"You've told me what I should do, but I still don't know which elements I need to use. I still don't know how to find out which things I need to balance."

"Take it from me," said the feng shui man. "You argue so much that I'd say you had a little too much Fire in your character."

"Do I?" I asked. "Or is it that I just can't make up my mind? Because if that's true then I've got too much Water. Or am I simply arguing because I'm an old stick-in-the-mud who doesn't want to change his ways? Because if *that's* true then I've obviously got too much Earth! See? We're still at square one!"

"Okay," said the feng shui man. "I'll tell you. You have a lot of Fire in your character, and a lot of Wood. That means you're hot-tempered, but keen on learning."

"Whatever," I said. "But how do you know that for sure?"

"Because," said the feng shui man, "you were born in 1986."

"What!?"

"1986," he grinned. "Fire and Wood, no doubt about it."

"Hang on! Have I missed something here? What difference does my age make?"

"It's not your age," he said. "It's the year you were born. The year of the Tiger."

"Tiger!?"

"I think," he said, "it's time I told you about Chinese astrology."

"I think," I yelled, "you should have told me hours ago!"

"See? Much too fiery."

The Chinese zodiac will tell you which element or elements were most important in your qi on the day you were born. Chinese horoscopes are a very complex issue, fully deserving a whole book to themselves, but I'm going to touch on the subject for a moment because it connects with the elements and colors in feng shui.

In olden days, Chinese people didn't have numbers for years. Instead they would have a cycle of 12 animals, and each year would be ruled by a different animal. This is the Chinese zodiac. Also, each year is ruled by one of the five elements, and the animal and element go together to determine what kind of person you will grow up to be. These two cycles only coincide once every 60 years, so the chances are quite high that every member of your family is ruled by a different combination of animal and element. It also means that the people you go to school with are likely to be ruled by the same combination of animal and element, because most of you were probably born in the same year.

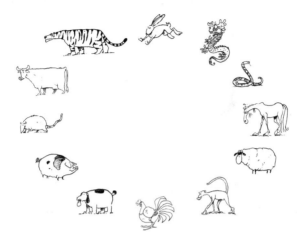

The next step is to find out your Chinese sign. The table on the next page lists all the years from 1964 to 2000, showing each year's ruling element, then that year's ruling animal, followed by the element that rules that animal. Find the year in which you were born and read along the table to find out which elements are already very much a part of your life. This will leave three or four elements that aren't already big features in your qi, and you might find that feng shui can help you to incorporate more of those elements into your life to bring you better fortune. Do bear in mind that the Chinese year follows a slightly different cycle to the Western one so, if you were born in January or early February, remember to check the day on which that year started—you might find that you belong to the sign of the year before. For instance, if you were born on January 20 1966, you belong to the year of the Snake whereas, if you were born on January 21 1966, you belong to the year of the Horse.

Year Starting	Year's Element	Year of The ...		Animal's Element	Double Trouble?
February 13 1964	Wood	Dragon		Earth	
February 2 1965	Wood	Snake		Fire	
January 21 1966	Fire	Horse		Fire	Y
February 9 1967	Fire	Sheep		Earth	
January 30 1968	Earth	Monkey		Metal	
February 17 1969	Earth	Rooster		Metal	
February 6 1970	Metal	Dog		Earth	
January 27 1971	Metal	Pig		Water	
February 15 1972	Water	Rat		Water	Y
February 3 1973	Water	Ox		Earth	
January 23 1974	Wood	Tiger		Wood	Y
February 11 1975	Wood	Rabbit		Wood	Y
January 31 1976	Fire	Dragon		Earth	
February 18 1977	Fire	Snake		Fire	Y
February 7 1978	Earth	Horse		Fire	
February 9 1979	Earth	Sheep		Earth	Y
February 16 1980	Metal	Monkey		Metal	Y
February 5 1981	Metal	Rooster		Metal	Y
January 25 1982	Water	Dog		Earth	

Year Starting	Year's Element	Year of The ...		Animal's Element	Double Trouble?
February 13 1983	Water	Pig		Water	Y
February 2 1984	Wood	Rat		Water	
February 20 1985	Wood	Ox		Earth	
February 9 1986	Fire	Tiger		Wood	
January 29 1987	Fire	Rabbit		Wood	
February 17 1988	Earth	Dragon		Earth	Y
February 6 1989	Earth	Snake		Fire	
January 27 1990	Metal	Horse		Fire	
February 15 1991	Metal	Sheep		Earth	
February 4 1992	Water	Monkey		Metal	
January 23 1993	Water	Rooster		Metal	
February 10 1994	Wood	Dog		Earth	
January 31 1995	Wood	Pig		Water	
February 19 1996	Fire	Rat		Water	
February 7 1997	Fire	Ox		Earth	
January 28 1998	Earth	Tiger		Wood	
February 16 1999	Earth	Rabbit		Wood	
February 5 2000	Metal	Dragon		Earth	

Double Trouble

There are some years in which the element that naturally rules a zodiac sign also rules that particular year. This can mean double trouble, and recent double-trouble years have included 1977, 1979, 1980, 1981, 1983, and 1988. What this means is that people born in that particular year will have an excess of the element that rules them, possibly enough to cause an imbalance.

For example, if you were born in 1988, the year of the Dragon, you will have Earth as the ruling element of your animal sign, and also as the ruling element of the year you were born. There's nothing wrong with this in itself, but you may find that sometimes you feel lazy and lethargic through carrying the weight of the world around with you. It's likely that brown and yellow will not be your lucky colors because there's already so much Earth in your soul. You might find that your situation improves if you combine your earthiness with another element. Adding the bright, lively reds of the Fire element to your clothes, room, or possessions might bring more zip into your life. Another way of dealing with this imbalance would be to wear more blacks and blues, because the neutralizing effect of Water would help to reduce some of the Earth. Try it and see.

Here's another example. If you were born in 1983, the year of the Pig, you will have entered the world in a double Water year. Pigs are naturally sensitive and easily hurt, but the double Water influence on your life may make you even more thin-skinned than others who share your sign. What you might need in your life is a little Earth, to make you calmer and not quite so wet. Earth will bring you strength, so perhaps surrounding yourself with browns and yellows might help.

Of course, you might find things harder to deal with if you have no control over the decor in your room. What do you do if, for example, you were born in 1985, the year of the Ox (Wood

and Earth), and find yourself living in a room with polished wooden floors, a green duvet on the bed, and yellow walls? The chances are quite high that you'll be overdosing on colors associated with Wood and Earth. You might find that you're a bit slow-witted or dull, or that other people are taking advantage of you. What you need is to bring a little more zip and savvy into your life, but you can't simply redecorate because your parents would have a complete fit. You can't change the walls, bedding, or floor, but you can compensate for them with pictures, objects, blankets, cushions, or even a rug. You can also adapt *yourself* through the colors you favor in your own clothes. The elements missing from your life (if you born in 1985, in this example) are Metal, Fire, and Water, which means that whites, reds, and blues in your room and about your person will help to balance the feng shui of your room, your life, and your luck.

The table below lists the ways in which elements can be used to strengthen, weaken and balance each other:

FIRE strengthens EARTH
because ash is left behind by fire.
EARTH strengthens METAL
because you have to mine underground for metals.
METAL strengthens WATER
because metal "sweats" (look at the outside of a cold drink can).
WATER strengthens WOOD
because you water your plants to make them grow.
WOOD strengthens FIRE
because it feeds the flames.

FIRE weakens METAL
because only heat will melt it.
METAL weakens WOOD
because metal makes the blades of saws and axes.
WOOD weakens EARTH
because tree roots push earth aside and sap its strength.
EARTH weakens WATER
because water soaks into the ground.
WATER destroys FIRE
obviously!

EARTH balances FIRE
because it can contain the flames.
METAL balances EARTH
because a metal shovel can move it around.
WATER balances METAL
because metal must temper itself or it gets rusty.
WOOD balances WATER
because it needs it to grow.
FIRE balances WOOD
because wood feeds the flames.

You can use colors, objects, and elements to make sure that weak sectors are stronger, overbearing sectors are weaker, and sectors that are just right remain just right.

You can also use objects and images that call your zodiac sign to life, either with representations of your zodiac sign, or by filling the room with things that would appeal to the real-life animal. Tigers and monkeys like forests, horses and sheep like fields, and so on. And if your animal is occasionally bullied by other creatures, remember to keep bad qi out of your life by avoiding them. A picture of a snake in a room occupied by someone born in the year of the Rat isn't going to go down very well, is it?

FOOD FOR THOUGHT: YOUR PERSONAL FENG SHUI

Now that we've been over most of the important rules, let's take a look at your personal feng shui profile. Get a piece of paper and note down the year of your birth. Check it against the chart to find out which elements are already important in your life. Which colors, shapes, and objects are used to represent those elements? Now write down the elements represented by the colors, shapes, and objects around you where you live. Are the various elements balanced or are they competing with each other? Does any one element dominate all the others? If so, which element do you need to counter its effect? Is there anything you can add to the room, or can you rearrange it, to balance things?

FOOD FOR THOUGHT: CHANGING YOUR FATE

Okay, let's assume that you've got your room all nice and balanced, and that your personal ruling elements and the elements around you are in perfect harmony. Your yin and yang are now in accord. You have, in effect, reached square one. Now it's time to try changing your fate by upsetting the balance again, but upsetting it in your favor. For this you will need to return to the magic octagon. Which areas of your life, luck, or fate do you think you need to alter?

If your room is balanced perfectly like a yin-yang seesaw, you can tip the scales of fate by using the sectors in the octagon. Perhaps you would like to be more understanding towards your friends. In that case, perhaps some Water colors, shapes, or objects in the northwest sector are what you need. The northwest rules helpful people, and Water rules your powers of understanding and adaptability.

Perhaps you want to encourage yourself to concentrate harder on your schoolwork. For that you'll need the northeast sector (knowledge and self-improvement). You'll need to improve this sector with Earth (for reliability), Wood (for perseverance), or perhaps Fire (to help you stay alert during those boring classes). You could also try a double-pronged attack by improving the northwest corner which, as you will see from the octagon, rules your head. You could help yourself to think more clearly with Water in this sector, or to think faster with Fire.

Maybe you're keener on improving your financial situation? For that, you'll need to concentrate on the wealth sector in the southeast. Strong, reliable Earth will stop you spending unwisely. Slow-but-sure Wood will help you to save up for something important, and Metal might bring you pennies from heaven, or money from an unexpected source. But Water and Fire would be bad for this area, because they might encourage you to fritter your money away and waste it on frivolities.

With the charts and tables in this book, it should be easy to improve your fate. With feng shui, the sky really is the limit.

CHAPTER 10

Bedroom Feng Shui

"Now we're cooking!" I said happily.

"Making sense, all of a sudden?" asked the feng shui man.

"Definitely. But ..."

"But what? I thought you understood everything?"

"Yeah, but I think it's a shame that I can't get the full benefit."

"Why not?"

"Because this isn't *my* house. It belongs to my parents, and they were born in different years, and we can't *all* balance the feng shui perfectly because we're ruled by different elements."

"True," said the feng shui man. "But you don't have to worry about the *whole* house, do you?"

"Don't I?"

"Of course not. You only have to worry about the part of the house that is yours and yours alone."

"Oh, right."

By now you've probably had a run-in with your parents after trying to convince them that they need an extra step for the patio, a new, curvy roof, and a new, feng shui-friendly location for the kitchen door. They've probably told you to shut up, because they are already aware of the teachings of Confucius. Confucius was very keen on ancestor

worship, which basically means you have to do whatever your parents tell you, otherwise a curse will be called down upon your house. So don't worry so much about your home—your parents will have to deal with any invading demons themselves.

There is one area of the house where you have a better say about the decoration and furniture, and that's your own room. The ancient feng shui manuals talk a lot about bedrooms, because their major purpose is to give you a good night's sleep.

Your room has special feng shui rules attached to it because, unlike an adult whose qi is affected by the entire house, you will spend a lot of time in this one area. You might do your homework here, or you might have a computer here which is for both work and play. If you have friends over, you will probably end up in your bedroom too. In other words, your bedroom is like a small house on its own. You work, play, sleep, and entertain there, so all the feng shui associated with an adult's bedroom, living room, and perhaps even office, are concentrated in this one small space.

For this reason, any feng shui rules you follow in your own room will be magnified in the rest of your life. It might be the only properly charmed room in your house, but for you personally it will have the effect of an entire adult mansion, perfectly organized along feng shui principles.

Unlucky Mess

Feng shui has very strict rules about untidiness, but they are extremely simple. An untidy room is very bad feng shui indeed. Clutter distracts you from going about your business. If trash accumulates in your room, it will attract evil spirits in exactly the same way that crumbs of food attract mice. If you ever see a dragon's lair, you will notice that there is not a single scrap of trash anywhere in sight. This is because the dragon's breath destroys anything that is in the way. For this reason, lucky dragons are reluctant to enter an untidy room, because they are afraid that their breath will set light to the trash and cause you harm. Encourage lucky dragons by keeping your room as tidy as possible.

If your room is an appalling mess at the moment, it will probably take a long while to put everything away in its proper place. But you will be amazed at how easy it is to keep it that way once you've tidied everything properly the first time. There is a knock-on effect with the rest of the house and family, too. You will find that your parents cause you less trouble, because they have one less thing to complain about. You will become more

confident because you know that if people come over they won't
be shocked to find you living like a pig in a sty. Your homework
will improve because you will know where everything is, and it
will be easier to do because you will have cleared a space to work
in, and you won't waste time scrabbling around in search of a
pen, a book, or more paper. If having a tidy room saves you five
minutes of wasted time every day, in a year that will add up to
over 30 hours of extra time. That's right, more than a whole day

of extra time for you to concentrate on enjoying yourself.

A tidy room is also easier to entertain guests in, and the Chinese are very keen on that. Chinese people are the best hosts in the world, because they always put the well-being of their guests first. In fact, one of the ways of saying "Hello" in Chinese translates as "Have you eaten yet?", because if you're their guest and you're hungry, it's their duty to see that you're well-fed and happy. As you must have realized by now from reading this book, the place where you live says a lot about you, not least because anyone who knows about feng shui can "read" your house's qi as easily as they can read a book. If you want your friends to return again and again, their time in your house should be stress-free and fun, and you can get things off to a good start by making sure that they don't keep tripping over the clutter in your room.

Sleeping Success

Windows and doors are yang areas, bright and loud with plenty of things happening outside, but if you want to be able to sleep properly it's best to locate your bed in one of the yin areas—in other words, against a wall that has no windows or doors. These areas are much calmer and darker, and will give you a better chance of sleeping soundly.

The bed should also be situated away from the door, and preferably on the other side of the room. This stops you being hit by any bad qi that might wander in through the door, and also allows you to keep an eye out for any evil spirits that may sneak in. If you can't place the bed that far away from the door, try hanging a mirror on the opposite wall so that you can still keep an eye on what's happening outside. Try to avoid sleeping near sharp corners or overhanging beams, because they might broadcast bad qi at you while you're asleep. If necessary, cover them over or hide them behind a softening object like a curtain, poster, or plant. The same applies to views outside the window. If your window shows a peaceful scene, such as trees or other greenery, then you have very good feng shui. If your window looks out over a dirty factory, parking lot, or busy road, it would be best to soften the view with some curtains or heavy drapes.

Last but not least for bed positioning, never sleep with your feet pointing towards the door. This is what is known as the Death Position, because this is the way that a body is laid out in a Chinese house before it leaves for the funeral. This is very bad feng shui indeed, but it is so simple to alter. Just put your pillow at the other end, and if you've been having bad luck recently, it should change for the better.

FOOD FOR THOUGHT: TWO BEDROOM EXAMPLES

This picture shows an excellent bedroom arrangement. It's not perfect, but that's because feng shui is all about dealing practically with what life sends our way. Note the rather unusual desk positioning. Instead of facing the wall and window (which would normally be fine), the desk has been turned around so it faces the door. Not only does the room's occupant now face the door, but he also gets all that lovely light streaming in through the window behind him. You will also notice that the desk is in the northeast sector, so it encourages knowledge and learning. The bed, of course, points the occupant's feet away from the door.

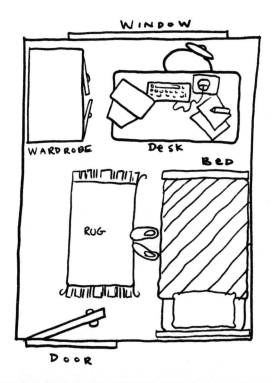

The other bedroom arrangement is very bad feng shui. Can you see why? First, the door opens straight on to the bed, directly opposite the sleeping sorcerer's feet. The desk, where all the work is done, letters are written, and computer games are played, is in a good position (facing the window), but also a bad position, because whoever is sitting at the desk can't see the door.

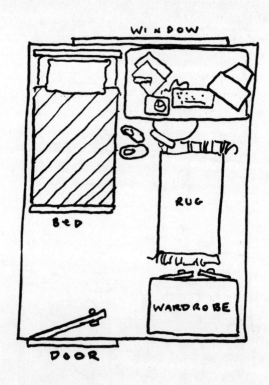

Bedroom Shrines

Your bedroom is also the ideal place to put up your favorite posters. The sight of the people (or perhaps places) on the posters will inspire you every day to be like them, but remember to follow the octagon rules. The best place to put a picture of a rock star is on the north wall (career, if you want to be a rock star too), south wall (fame, if you want to be as well known), or perhaps southeast (wealth, if you want to be as rich as one). But ask yourself exactly what it is that you love about your heroes or heroines, and take care that you don't accidentally get more than you bargained for. Suppose you stuck up a picture of King Henry VIII (silly example, I know, but bear with me), hoping that he would become your guardian spirit and help you to become very rich and powerful. Just make sure you don't put the picture in the southwest (marriage) part of your room, otherwise you'll be doomed to follow his bad luck in marriage.

You should also be careful with pictures of movie stars. Do you want to be like the actor or actress, or like the person that he or she is playing in the picture? Places are easier. Is there anywhere you've always wanted to visit? Try pinning up a picture of it in the northwest (travel) part of your room, and who knows what your luck might bring you?

Sibling Rivalry

Don't forget that the feng shui principles designed to deter burglars and evil spirits can also keep unwelcome visitors out of your room. Imagine that your brothers or sisters are sneaking into your room, and think of the many ways you can make them feel uneasy or trick them into slinking away guiltily, leaving your diary unread and your clothes unborrowed:

◆✦ A mirror so they are startled by the sight of their own reflection.

◆✦ A bell, wind chimes, or similar device on the door so that their entry makes a noise.

◆✦ A room so tidy that you will easily notice the disturbance made when any object is moved.

Any of the above methods might be enough on its own to discourage a meddlesome invader, be it a ghost or something more mundane like a nosy member of your family. Tidiness itself should be a good parent-deterrent, since they will have one less reason to barge in and complain at you.

Stuck in the Middle

You might have to share a room with one of your siblings. Let's assume that half of the room is yours and the other half belongs to your brother or sister. If you're both studying feng shui there probably won't be any problems. If you're not, then you'll have to arrange your half of the room in two ways. The first is as discussed above, to ensure good feng shui for yourself. The other way is to protect yourself from any bad feng shui being broadcast by your sibling. If your sibling has plenty of objects with sharp corners, or posters on the walls that send bad qi in your direction, you will have to insulate yourself with some of the usual charms. Mobiles, mirrors, or plants in the right location will protect you from your sibling's inadvertent bad qi.

Others may find themselves having to sleep in bunkbeds. If your sibling doesn't believe in feng shui, try to convince him or her to let you have the lower bunk, because it will be in the shadow of the upper bed and hence a better yin area for restful

sleep. You will also be in a better place to attract good qi while asleep, because most top bunks can only be reached by a stepladder, which good qi will find very difficult to climb.

THE STORY SO FAR

◆✦ You didn't buy your house so, when all is said and done, its feng shui is not your problem.

◆✦ Because you spend so much time in your bedroom, it is the crucial center of your feng shui.

◆✦ Use the octagon and feng shui rules in this book to improve your bedroom qi.

◆✦ Treat invading siblings as hostile demons, and scare them off with the usual methods.

A BEDROOM FENG SHUI CHECKLIST

Room shape	Beware of sharp corners.
Portals	Doors, windows, and fireplaces are all powerful influences on their sectors.
View	What can you see from the window?
Walls	Color.
Decoration	Posters, pictures, etc.
Color	Of other areas, such as the carpet, floor, bedspread.
Bed placement	Yin area, feet away from the door.
Objects	Desks, chairs, tables, shelves, books, plants, photographs, just about anything.
Your personal feng shui profile	Are your strong/weak elements balanced?
Your own wishes	Which octagon sectors do you want to improve?

Feng Shui at School

The Chinese place immense value on learning. It's a matter of luck if your parents are rich or your father is the Emperor, but anyone can become great by learning from his or her elders.

In old China, the only way to get a good job was to pass the government exams, which were more than just a couple of hours in a drafty hall answering questions. In fact, they often took several days. Candidates were locked in little rooms with the test

papers, a few snacks, and a portable potty, and weren't allowed out until they had finished. The exams were fiendishly difficult, and some of the students even went mad. And as if that wasn't bad enough, every single qualification had a sell-by date. You had to do the exams again every few years, otherwise you would lose your grade.

With such difficult and demanding examinations, it's only natural that the Chinese should have thought about making educational life easier. One candidate tried to tattoo all the answers on his body, but forgot he would have to take his clothes off before he could read them! The Chinese are not impressed by cheaters. They aren't even that impressed by people who are naturally talented. If you are talented anyway, they say, then what's so clever about doing what comes naturally? The only thing that really impresses the Chinese is good, old-fashioned, hard work. Of course, that's not to say that a little sorcery can't come into it as well.

Lucky Directions

In ancient China, the best students got the chance to go to the capital and work for the Emperor. And since the capital, Beijing, is in the northeast of China, the northeast became the feng shui direction of learning. You will see from your octagon that the northeast also rules the hand, because that's the part of you that has to do all the writing.

As usual, you can't control the way that your school was built, and it's probably been there for a lot longer than you. But you can use feng shui to make your life at school easier. Most classrooms, even in the barbarian West, are designed with feng shui principles in mind. The door is normally at the front of the room, placed so that the first thing you see is the teacher's desk. This is very good feng shui for education, because it reminds the students that they have come to the class to learn from their teacher, and not to play games or eat ice cream. Some schools also have the teacher's desk or lectern set on a podium, so that knowledge can fall from the teacher's brain and into the students' heads.

Classroom Feng Shui

Take a look at the picture, which shows a typical classroom where the seating arrangements demonstrate feng shui principles.

The front, where the teacher is standing, is at the north end. The smart feng shui sorcerers will sit in the northeast section, so that knowledge and learning come effortlessly to them. But woe betide those class members who don't understand the principles of magic. In the southern part of the classroom we have two class clowns who spend all their time misbehaving. They think they're really clever, of course, because they're sitting in the fame part of the class octagon. Everybody in the class knows who they are, but they're not learning anything. Neither are the girls in the southwest corner, who are far away from the teacher's attention and spend all their time brushing their hair and checking their fingernails. This is because they are sitting in the marriage sector. If they really want to get ahead in life, they should be sitting with the sorcerers in the northeast, or at the front (north) which is the career sector. Note that one of the pupils is in the same sector as the teacher's desk, which is the northwest (helpful people) sector. This is also quite a lucky place to sit, because the teacher will give this pupil extra-special attention, but this pupil will have to help the teacher in return by volunteering to hand out books and keep the classroom tidy. If you sit here, be careful that you don't start to cause negative qi among your friends by appearing to be the teacher's pet. (Chinese people consider it an honor to be the teacher's pet. The way in which the rest of your class regard it will depend on how many barbarians there are. In a perfect world, everyone in your class would be a feng shui master and then everyone would be the teacher's pet!)

Who knows whether all these people were like that in the beginning? Maybe they sat there because that's the kind of persons they are, and they were simply drawn to the part of the classroom where they naturally belonged. But it's equally possible that they *became* that way because they chose to sit where they did. Perhaps those children who clown around at the back might be model students if they sat closer to the front. Perhaps those children who are always talking in the western side of the classroom might quieten down if they moved closer to the qi center of the classroom. Who knows? All we can say for sure is that it's easy to spot the feng shui sorcerers in this classroom because they'll be right up at the front where knowledge just streams into their brain. This means they don't have to work hard to catch up with the lessons or study, because they find it easy to remember things the first time they hear them.

Other Classroom Layouts

If your classroom is an odd shape, such as an L-shape, try not to sit in the shadow of the "L," or in any seat where bad qi from the sharp wall will point in your direction. If you can't avoid this, hang your coat over the back of your chair to insulate you from the nasty vibes floating towards you.

It is very bad feng shui to sit with your back to the door. Originally this was because it made it easier for marauders and evil spirits to sneak up on you, but at school there is another problem. If your classroom has an entrance at the back, whoever sits closest to it will have bad luck. The door behind you will always be a distraction. There will be noises from outside, and perhaps even a draft that takes your mind off your work. The person who sits at the back of this kind of classroom can always be the first out of the door, the last into the classroom, and the last person to catch the teacher's attention. Sitting near the back door encourages the student to spend more time thinking about what happens after class, instead of concentrating on the lesson, so try to avoid it.

Some classrooms, especially for younger children, have the pupils sitting around tables facing each other. This is all very well, especially if your table is in the knowledge sector of the classroom, but try to make sure that you sit facing the teacher. If you find yourself naturally sitting with your back towards the teacher, you will have to keep twisting and turning to hear what your teacher is saying, which means that you will have to *strain* to learn anything. Make school life easier for yourself and sit so you can see the teacher at all times.

Another classroom arrangement is the lecture hall, where the teacher stands at the bottom of a pit and the students sit on steps that rise away from him or her. This is very bad feng shui for learning, and is best avoided. The teacher's knowledge must rise up towards the students, turning the task of teaching them anything at all into an uphill struggle. Meanwhile, the students are sitting in an arrangement not unlike that at the movies or in a theater. They expect to be entertained! These classes might be fun, but they won't be very useful as education.

FOOD FOR THOUGHT: YOUR SCHOOL'S FENG SHUI

Schools come in all shapes and sizes, but what does the layout of your school say about it? Try walking around your school to see how it was designed. My brother's school is really unusual. It has two main blocks of classrooms, joined by a long corridor. Halfway down the corridor is the entrance and secretarial office at the front, and the main assembly hall at the back. Then there's the handicraft block, which is a new building bolted unceremoniously on to the back and contains all the woodwork and metalwork classrooms. Add all that up and what do you get? When you see the school from above it looks just like a scorpion! The assembly hall is the body, the secretaries' office is the head, the two classroom blocks are the pincers and the handicraft annex is the poisonous tail. It all sounds rather scary, but since my brother's school is in a tough neighborhood, it needs to look dangerous to scare away the demons!

Some schools are much more open plan and, since many of them have become too small for the number of kids who go there, a lot have prefab huts dotted around the perimeter to take the overflow of students. These can be bad news for education feng shui, because if it's raining and you have to trudge through the storm to reach your next class, you'll end up walking into the classroom all soggy and miserable, which is hardly a good way to begin. There's no real way of stopping the rain, but you can plan ahead to improve things. If you think it might rain that day, why not take an umbrella with you to make the journey between classes drier? Not only will you have less trouble settling in at the start of the class, the chances are quite high that a lot of people will suddenly want to be your friend for the march through the rain.

Some schools, often in crowded cities, are in a single story block, surrounded by the playground and in turn by a high wall. This makes them like castles, with the playground working as a moat. But a moat of what? A moat of fun, to insulate the school building from the miserable city outside? Perhaps. Look at your own school layout and try to decide what the architects had in mind when they designed it. Were your school's architects thinking about the principles of feng shui, or were they simply mad? If you were designing a school along feng shui principles, how would you improve it? How could you use the octagon to get the maximum benefit from lessons? A gym in the east sector (for health), with most of the classrooms in the north and northeast? Where would you put the staffroom to turn the teachers into friendlier people? What about the library and the dining hall? And what color would you want to paint the whole building? Most schools are painted with drab, neutral colors like snot-green and pus-yellow; if you were in charge, what do you think would make school more fun for everyone? Don't forget, by the way, that most of the people in each class will have been born in the same year, so will share the same ruling elements. Have any of the teachers caught on to this and put up pictures and objects in their classrooms to help balance their students? Is there a particularly unruly class in your school that could benefit from a little careful yin-yang balancing on their walls? Or is that class particularly badly behaved for another reason? Perhaps their front door opens into one end of a long corridor, so all the bad qi zooms down in straight lines and straight into their brains.

FOOD FOR THOUGHT: THE WORLD HASN'T CHANGED ... YOU HAVE!

Ask yourself these questions and more, and keep on asking. Now you know all about feng shui, you can start looking with new eyes at every building and room you see. Every house or shop has its own unique feng shui, so see if you can spot what's right or wrong in each case. Every person you meet will come from a different feng shui situation. Are they happy or sad? Fast or slow? Smart or stupid? Friendly or nasty? And if so, how has their feng shui affected their qi? This book should have given you a different way of looking at the world, and a different way of looking at yourself. Keep on experimenting until you like what you see.

CHAPTER 12

Back to the Real World

So now you've taken your first steps on the long, winding path of feng shui sorcery. I hope since you started reading this book you've begun to look at the world in a different way. The world never changes, but sometimes people do, and it's the job of the feng shui sorcerer to keep changing, to keep learning, and never to forget that we live in a permanent whirl of qi. We are all connected by wind and water to the world around us. Everything we do affects other people, and everything they do affects us.

That is the fundamental lesson of feng shui, that we should treat others as we'd like them to treat us, and do our best to bring good qi into the world for everyone. Feng shui is not about putting curses on people you don't like, or ruining their qi by switching their posters around on the wall. It's about living a good, happy life for yourself, so that you find yourself living to a ripe old age, surrounded by the love of your children and the

laughter of your descendants. And it all starts here, with you being kind to your ancestors, on the lookout for dragons in disguise, and polite to the local spirits.

"So that's it?" I asked.
"Oh, no," said the feng shui man. "That's only the beginning."
"So why are you packing up?"
"I've got things to do," said the feng shui man. "And so have

you, kid. Your room's a dreadful mess, your bed needs moving, that poster on your wall needs to be replaced by something more calming, and if I were you I'd get your parents to put a brighter lightbulb in your room so you can read better at night."

"And if I do all that, my luck will change?"

"Haven't you listened to a word I've been saying?"

"Yes, but ... I'm still not sure it'll work."

"You'll never know until you try," he said, shutting his case with a snap. "Feng shui is not just an art, it's a science as well, so there's no harm in experimenting until you find something that works best for you."

"So where are you going now?" I asked.

"I'm off to tell your great-grandmother how you're doing," he said with a wink. "She told me you'd be hard to convince." He stood on the front step and sniffed at the air.

"What is it?" I asked.

"It's going to rain," he said.

"How can you tell?"

"Can't you feel the qi in the air? It's whipping around like there's no tomorrow. And look at the sky ... so dark and full of clouds. Of course it's going to rain."

"Wow!" I said. "Does that mean there will be dragons in the air tonight?"

"Perhaps."

"Hang on," I said. "I'll get you an umbrella."

"That's very kind," he shouted after me as I bolted upstairs. Perfect! If I lent him an umbrella, he'd have to bring it back and I could find out more about feng shui.

But as I was running back down clutching an old umbrella, I heard the front door slam. I pulled it open and dashed out into the front yard, but the feng shui man was nowhere to be seen.

Just then, the rain started coming down in buckets, and I opened the umbrella to keep dry. I thought I saw the feng shui man out of the corner of my eye, but when I turned to look he'd disappeared. There was a flash of lightning up above, swiftly followed by a monstrous clap of thunder.

"Wow!" I said to no one in particular.

I turned to go back inside, the rain spattering down around me like the beating of a thousand wings.

Glossary of

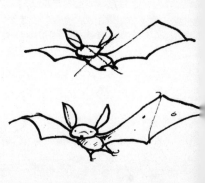

Magical Influences

Glossary of Magical Influences

To make practical feng shui a little easier for you, this book finishes with a glossary of many items which, although they appear to be everyday objects, work as qi magnets and should help you in the planning of your feng shui. Also included is a much wider selection of other lucky charms and ideas.

With the aid of this book, your magic octagon, and this glossary, you should be able to rearrange the qi situation of your home and life so that more luck comes to you.

But remember, the feng shui sorcerers are resourceful and thoughtful. If something doesn't work, experiment. Feng shui has worked for 3,000 years and, if you want it to work *for you*, you may have to work *with it* for a while.

Air-conditioning
Cool, and therefore a yin influence.

Art
A picture of an object has the

same magical value as having the object itself in the room.

Bamboo

Bamboo remains green all year round, and is also known for bending with the wind and the elements. For this reason, it is the symbol of long life, endurance, and adaptability. When the wind blows through a bamboo grove, the rubbing of the stems makes a moaning sound thought to be the wailing of ghosts. Consequently, the use of bamboo in the home is said to ward off evil spirits.

Bat

Hangs upside down so brings a different perspective to your thoughts. Good for encouraging you to think in new and original ways.

Bells

The ringing of a bell opens a pathway to heaven and scares away evil spirits. Also works as a guardian spirit because a bell can be an alarm.

Black

The color of night, deep water, and mystery. Can also represent a new beginning.

Blue

The color of the sky and water. Represents truth, honor, and spiritualism.

Books

Bring knowledge and encourage study. Holy books are particularly strong charms against demons.

Bridges

Symbols of communication and travel, and of reaching out to people. But try not to spend too much time in the middle of a bridge. Because it is halfway between A and B, it is Nowhere, and hence a favorite haunt of ghosts.

Brown

The color of earth, security, and solid foundations.

Butterfly

Represents the soul of someone who has just died. Also the spirit of joy and happiness.

Chrysanthemum

Flower symbolizing joy, happiness, and an easy life.

Clouds

Symbols of heaven and achievement. The sky's the limit …

Coins

Symbols of money and financial success.

Crane

Bird symbolizing long life and purity. Also represents justice, because Chinese judges used to have crane symbols in their courtrooms.

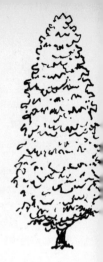

Cypress
An evergreen tree, and therefore a symbol
of youth and vigor.

Deer
Animal symbolizing immortality because
in Chinese legend it
found the fungus of
eternal youth.

Dog
Sign of the Chinese zodiac.
A friend and protector to
everyone, but also prone to
being permanently on guard
and defensive even of those

things that don't need to be defended.

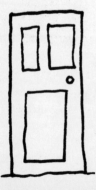

Door
The area of a room that contains the door is the
most important sector in
that room's octagon, because the door is the
portal between your current
location and the rest of the universe.

Dragon
Sign of the Chinese zodiac. Great strength and courage, a powerful protector, and bringer of cleansing rains and vengeful thunderstorms. Can fly without wings and hence symbolizes success without effort. The most powerful symbol of good luck, and also of the Emperor.

Duck
Happiness and faithfulness, especially in marriage. A symbol of romance and undying love.

Electrical objects
Great providers of yang energy to brighten a room and cheer up the occupants. Radios, TVs, computers, etc., put out noise and color, and are symbols of happiness and friendship.

Elephant
Symbol of strength, wisdom, and long memory. Powerful protectors of graves.

Flowers

Any flowers bring bright, happy qi with their perfume, good for cheering up sad people and helping people who are ill.

Fountains

Soothing waters and bringers of money (see water).

Goldfish

Good fortune in the future. Goldfish can also be used as conductors of bad qi. Some feng shui masters say that if a pet goldfish dies, it has absorbed all the bad qi that would otherwise have caused a terrible accident for a family member. Rumored to turn into a dragon when it passes through the gates of Heaven.

Green

The color of calm. In the US it can be a symbol of money, because of the color of the dollar bill. Represented by the east in the magic octagon, and hence a symbol of the family and health. Too much green in your life may cause you to become a jealous person.

Gray

A mixture of black and white, and hence a symbol of confusion and falsehood. A symbol 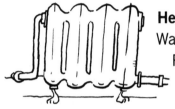 of biding one's time, waiting for the moment to pounce. A symbol of nothing special, and hence a good color for spies and others hoping to remain unnoticed.

Heating

Warm and cozy, so a yang object. Radiators, electric heaters, and similar appliances can help to reduce the yin overload in cold rooms.

Heavy objects

Symbols of solidity and confidence. Too many indicate an inability to listen to reason or to others' opinions.

Horse

Sign of the Chinese zodiac. Likable and hardworking, but also occasionally tactless, selfish, and obstinate. Symbol of speed and endurance. Noble and trustworthy.

Jade

A gift from Heaven to Earth. Many Chinese people like to wear jade lucky charms, but insist that the charms only work if they are received as a gift from someone else. If you buy jade for yourself, it won't work. Jade can be broken but never twisted, so has become a symbol of steadfastness, honor, and heroism. If your jade charm shatters, it means that it has deflected a demonic attack and saved you from a nasty accident.

Lights

Great for brightening up a room with yang energy and for scaring away evil spirits.

Lotus

A beautiful flower which grows in muddy pools, and hence a symbol of purity, glory, and triumph over hard times. Used inside houses to represent peace.

Magnolia

Flower symbolizing sweetness and the ability to charm others.

Mirror

All-purpose feng shui tool for deflecting demons, brightening and extending rooms, warding against sharp corners, and checking for vampires. Also used for entrapping evil spirits and making sure that ladies have their mascara on properly. Very useful, but avoid placing two mirrors facing each other because the long "corridor" stretching into infinity can become a hallway to hell at certain times of the year.

Mobiles

Work like silent wind chimes, brightening rooms and keeping the qi moving around. This helps to prevent qi becoming stale.

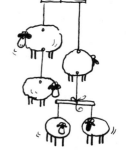

Monkey

Sign of the Chinese zodiac. Lively and quick-witted, but also prone to being too playful at the expense of hard work.

Octagon

Eight-sided magical symbol used to divide a room into sectors. Each sector rules a different part of your life, and can be balanced and enhanced with the aid of charms and colors.

Orange

Color of the sun at sunset and hence a symbol of reluctance to get on with something. Color of sociability, although too much of it will make you a follower rather than a leader. The fruit, as opposed to the color, symbolizes luck and, because of the color, represents gold and wealth. In Hong Kong, it also means money because the word for "orange" sounds similar to the word for "money" in Cantonese.

Orchid

Flower symbolizing love and good taste.

Ox

Sign of the Chinese zodiac. Hardworking and uncomplaining, they enjoy helping others, but can sometimes be stubborn and slow.

Peaches

Fruit said to grow in the garden of Heaven, and therefore a symbol of immortality.

Pear

Symbol of long life, because the pear tree flourishes for many years.

Peony

Known as the "King of Flowers" to the Chinese, it brings luck (especially in love) but also financial success and honor.

Persimmon

Its bright color makes it a symbol of happiness.

Phoenix

Symbol of peace, happiness, and long marriage. Said to grant children to childless couples. Because it burns itself to rise from the ashes in a better state, it is also a representation of the endless striving for perfection.

Pig

Sign of the Chinese zodiac. Sensitive and caring, sometimes too much so because they are easily hurt.

Pine

Pine trees remain evergreen, so are a symbol of eternal youth. In some parts of Asia, they are also a symbol of faithful love.

Plants

All plants can be used to soften sharp edges in a room, and thus reduce bad qi.

Plum

The plum tree produces flowers even in advanced old age, and so is a symbol of a long and productive life.

Pomegranate

Symbol of a large, faithful, and successful family.

Purple

Color worn by artists and writers, hermits and saints. Symbol of passion, love, and truth, but also of suffering if used to excess.

Qi

The breath of the universe and the raw material of life and fortune. Good qi likes soft curves and slow movement, bad qi zips around in straight lines and sharp corners.

Rabbit

Sign of the Chinese zodiac. Lucky and ambitious, the Rabbit sometimes bites off more than it can really chew. Symbol of long life and quick thinking. A red hare is a symbol of good luck.

Rat

Sign of the Chinese zodiac, great at advising others but bad at making up their own minds. Honest and resourceful, but sometimes also greedy.

Red

Color of fire, marriage, and good luck. If used too much, it can lead to hot tempers and bad moods.

Rooster

Sign of the Chinese zodiac. This creature has a crown on his head for nobility, and spurs on his feet for courage. The watchful eye he keeps on the chickens makes him a symbol of guardianship, and his early morning wake-up call makes him a symbol of reliability. Sometimes gets too courageous, risking foolhardiness and arrogance.

Sheep

Sign of the Chinese zodiac. Kindhearted and successful in business, they can be indecisive and often need a shepherd to keep them in line.

Snake

Sign of the Chinese zodiac. Wise, hypnotic, and elegant, but sometimes selfish and also liable to strike first if tormented. Can be a bit of a show-off.

Spinning things

Anything that rotates, which includes music boxes, tape and CD players, old-fashioned clocks with hands, and revolving doors. Good for stimulating helpful qi.

Tiger

Sign of the Chinese zodiac. Born leaders, they don't take orders happily. The Tiger is a fierce creature that can scare demons and humans alike. An excellent protector, but take care if there are new arrivals in your household and you have representations of one or more tigers on your walls. Tigers might mistake those born in the year of the Rooster, Rabbit, or Pig for food.

Toys

Childish things, and hence likely to make you seem a bit of a baby. If you want to be treated like an adult, keep them tucked out of sight, if you want to be regarded as a big kid (which can be useful sometimes) keep them in full view.

Trash

General household trash smells bad and attracts vermin, two properties guaranteed to attract bad qi. Trash is best kept outside the house, and interior trash cans are best kept lidded and clean at all times. Untidiness is also bad for feng shui, because kind dragons are put off from fear of igniting the mess inadvertently.

Trash can/wastepaper basket

Must be placed in a strong sector of your octagon otherwise it will bring bad luck to an area you are already weak in.

Trees

Excellent for blocking bad qi and softening sharp corners. Also a symbol of the Wood element, for obvious reasons.

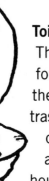

Toilet

The water aspect makes this a mini-pond for feng shui purposes, but what goes into the toilet is human waste, and therefore trash (bad qi). The toilet, as well as any other drain or disposal chutes, functions as an extra door that leads out of your house, and can "flush away" qi of all kinds, both good and bad. For this reason, bathrooms and kitchens should always be well-lit and full of good objects, especially mirrors and sweet-smelling things like room fresheners and soaps.

Tortoise

Symbol of a long and healthy life, and also of slow but steady growth.

Unicorn

Gentle symbol of wise rulership in a time of peace, also of famous children. Very useful for parents, especially placed in the west part of their abode (children sector).

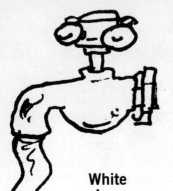

Water

Excellent element for encouraging good qi and absorbing the bad. Too much will make you indecisive and oversensitive.

White

Symbol of purity and innocence, as in the white belt worn by novice martial artists. Also the symbol of the element Metal and of mourning. A very yang color, because white reflects light and works as a weak mirror.

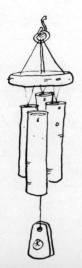

Wind chimes

A place for wandering spirits to rest during the night, and an effective alarm during the day. They create soothing sounds and protection from burglars.

Windows

Observation portals to the outside world, these let in yang essence and good qi. Watch for those things you can see through the window, as they will influence your life in the same way as if they were inside the room itself. Block nasty views with drapes, curtains, or objects on the windowsill.

Yang

All that is bright and loud. Invigorating.

Yellow

Symbol of the Emperor, also of earth because of the yellowish tinge of the soil in parts of China.

Yin

All that is dark and quiet. Calming.